WELCOME TO BARNET

A guide to the town of Barnet.
The only location in London where a battle from the War of the Roses has ever taken place! Together with its by-gone past, we believe that Barnet is the most historic town in the whole of London. Read on and you will discover just why!

Written by Brian Carroll for the Barnet Tourist Board
© 2024

Barnet is situated in the county of Hertfordshire on the northern outskirts of the Borough of Barnet. There are three Barnet's; High (Chipping) Barnet, New Barnet and East Barnet, which is also known as the village. Barry Swain and Brian Carroll set up The Barnet Tourist Board in the summer of 2019. with the intention of attracting visitors to their town. They consider Barnet to be probably the most historic town in London, naturally, outside of the actual ancient City of London itself!

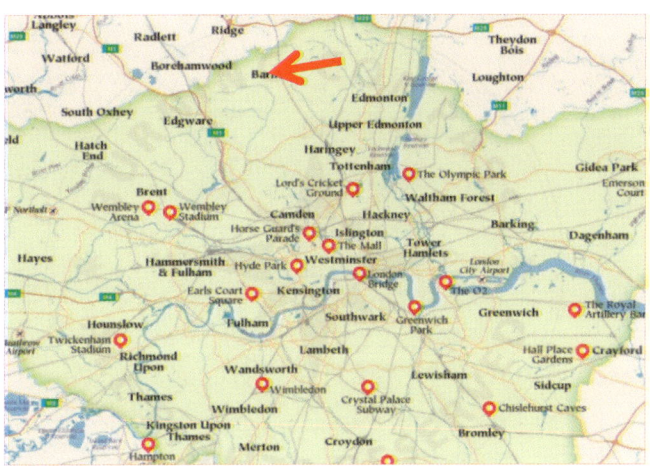

For instance, did you know that Barnet has 11th, 12th and 13th century churches, a couple of 16th century public houses, the site where Oliver Twist met the Artful Dodger in the classic novel by Charles Dickens (who also used to frequent the local taverns in the town)? They also have the 16th century Tudor Hall that was founded by Elizabeth 1st and the home of David Livingstone, the famous explorer, (Doctor Livingstone I presume) who also happens to be featured on the cover of the Beatle's album, "Sergeant Pepper's Lonely Hearts Club Band". There is naturally so much more to tell.

If the site of the Battle of Barnet was found Barnet would change overnight with tourist from not just this country but also the world.
The Barnet Tourist Board is also working on this with their publication of "In search of the battlefield" which relates the research we have put into this centuries old mystery. Available on Amazon.
So here is a tour around our town and a bit of history on the way.
Hope you enjoy Barnet.

CONTENTS

CHIPPING BARNET	Page 6
NEW BARNET	Page 10
EAST BARNET	Page 12
HADLEY	Page 14
BARNET HILL	Page 16
BARNET CHURCH	Page 19
LONDONS MAIN COACHING STOP	Page 21
TALLY-HO!" TO BARNET by Richard Selby	Page 22
BARNET PUBS.	Page 27
BYGONE PUBS IN BARNET.	Page 29
TUDOR HALL.	Page 34
BARNET MUSEUM	Page 36
CYRIL FRISBY	Page 37
THE BATTLE of BARNET	Page 38
WHERE ARE THE BODIES BURIED?	Page 43
WOULD THE BATTLE MAKE A GOOD FILM?	Page 45
BARNET MARKET	Page 49
BARNET FAIR	Page 53
THE BARNET RACES	Page 56
BARNET ROAD SIGNS	Page 58
HADLEY CHURCH	Page 62
THE GHOST OF OAKHILL PARK	Page 63
GENERAL MONCK'S VISIT TO BARNET	Page 65
THE OLD PHYSIC WELL	Page 67
DAVID LIVINGSTONE	Page 70
OLIVER TWIST MEETS THE ARTFUL DODGER	Page 72
THE LOCAL CINEMAS	Page 76
BIRT ACRES (1854 - 1918)	Page 79
LOTTE REINIGER (1899-1981)	Page 81
WHERE DID THE BOMBS DROP IN BARNET	Page 83
WHY BOMB BARNET	Page 85
ARKLEY VIEW AND THE RADIO SECURITY SERVICE.	Page 87
DID CHURCHILL MEET HESS IN WHETSTONE?	Page 90
BARNET PARKS AND OPEN SPACES	Page 93
HIGHLAND GARDENS	Page 96
HISTORY of THE BULL HEATRE	Page 98
THE WARREN THEATRE	Page 100
SIR ALEXANDER CUMING (1691 – 1775)	Page 101
SPIKE MILLIGAN	Page 103
BARNET FOOTBALL CLUB	Page 105
JOHN MOTSON.	Page 107
WHO'S WHO around Barnet	Page 109
101 THINGS ABOUT BARNET?	Page 119

BARNET TIME LINE

1070. Barnet known as "Barnetto".
12th Century. High Barnet founded by monks from St Albans Abbey.
1196. Barnet known as "Bernet".
1199. King John granted Barnet a market charter.
1250. Chapel built on site of Barnet Church.
1219. Barnet known as "Barnatt".
1249. First reference to East Barnet.
1291. Population of Barnet about 350.
1329. First reference to Chipping Barnet.
1349. Black Death kills 84 residents.
1420. St Johns Church (Barnet Church) was extended.
1471. Battle of Barnet during the Wars of the Roses.
1573. Q.E. Grammar school founded.
1577. Tudor Hall built.
1588. Barnet Fair and market granted a charter by Queen Elizabeth I.
17th Century. Great North Road built through Barnet. It was the main coach route from London to Scotland.
1667. Samuel Pepys visits the Barnet physic well.
1740. The Hadley Highstone obelisk is erected.
1758. Market day is changed from Monday to Wednesday. Fair changed from April to September.
1784. First stage coach service through Barnet.
1826. The St Albans Road built.
1827. Barnet Hill built.
1850. Great Northern Railway Company builds New Barnet Station.
1870. The last horse race in Barnet, "The Barnet Stakes" was held where High Barnet station now stands.
1873. Oakleigh Park Station opens.
1913. The Barnet Cinema built (On the site of the current Post Office in the High Street).
1935. Lorry kills four people at Barnet Fair.
1940. High Barnet station becomes part of the London Underground.
1965. Chipping Barnet becomes a part of the London Borough of Barnet.
1969. Hadley Brewery closes down.
1989. Spires shopping centre opens.

THE EARLY YEARS

CHIPPING BARNET.

In Saxon times Barnet was part of an extensive wood called Southaw, belonging to the Abbey of St Albans.

There have been a couple of theories about how the town got its name as it appears in early deeds as Bergnet, the Saxon word signifying a monticules or little hill while others believe it comes from the Saxon word, Baernet, meaning 'the place cleared by burning'.

Whichever one is true, it was the belief of the older natives that "Barnet stands on the highest ground betwixt London and York."

It is known that Chipping, meaning 'the market' was added to the town in 1199, when permission was granted to the Abbot of St Albans by King John to hold a weekly market in Barnet.

The population of the manor of Barnet in 1348 numbered a mere 350 of which many residents died in the Black Death. Just over a hundred years later there were six pubs in the town and thousands of thirsty soldiers after a battle on Hadley Common.

There are many historical buildings in the Barnet area, one of which is Tudor Hall next to Barnet College in Wood Street.

This hall was built in 1577 and was used as Queen Elizabeth's Grammar School for Boys. It is the oldest known building in Chipping Barnet today.

In 1667 Pepys enjoyed "some of the best cheesecakes that ever I ate in my life" at the Red Lion. (Which was situated by Tapster Street)

With the coming of the stage coach Barnet became one of the most important towns in the country with 150 horse drawn vehicles coming and going through the town every day. The smell must have been awful but they probably had lovely roses!

In 1762 author William Toldervy wrote that *'Chipping Barnet consists chiefly of one street, in which are some good inns, particularly the Mitre and Red Lion'.* Sometime later, Charles Dickens (whose meal at the Red Lion had once been cut short by the news that his wife had given birth to a daughter) described Oliver Twist limping into Barnet and' crouching on a step for some time wondering at the great number of public houses, ("*every other house in Barnet was a tavern, large or small*").

There were a number of inns in the High Street to cater for those coming into or going out of London that took care of the needs of travelers on the road, as well as the horses and drivers of the coaches. The Mitre inn existed in 1633 and is possibly the oldest remaining coaching inn building although the Kings Head is the oldest pub.

The life size model of the lion we see today at The Red Lion was added in the Victorian period and was kept when the pub was rebuilt in 1931.

Like the Mitre the Red Lion was a coaching inn, and there was stout competition between establishments for customers; particularly the Red Lion and the Green Man.

It was not unknown for fights between the ostlers of these two inns. *The ostlers were the men who would take care of the traveler's horses. Before Barnet Hill was built you would have to get into the town via Victoria Lane, which runs down the side of part of the old Barnet College. The lane is now cut short, but it used to run down to the Mays Lane and Red Lion at Underhill. In 1818 work was started on a road which was less steep and which we still use today.

This is an old picture of Mays Lane with the Red Lion in view. This would have been the route into Barnet.

The new road allowed armies to move more swiftly along it. Another difficulty for travelers using the Great North Road at Barnet was a section locally known as the squeeze, and because it was never corrected it is still visible today where the road passes between the Kings Head, and St John the Baptist.

The squeeze used to be longer, as a number of shops, which occupied an island in the middle of the road in front of the church. These shops were called Middle Row and were the original location of the Barnet market. Middle Row was demolished after a fire in 1889.

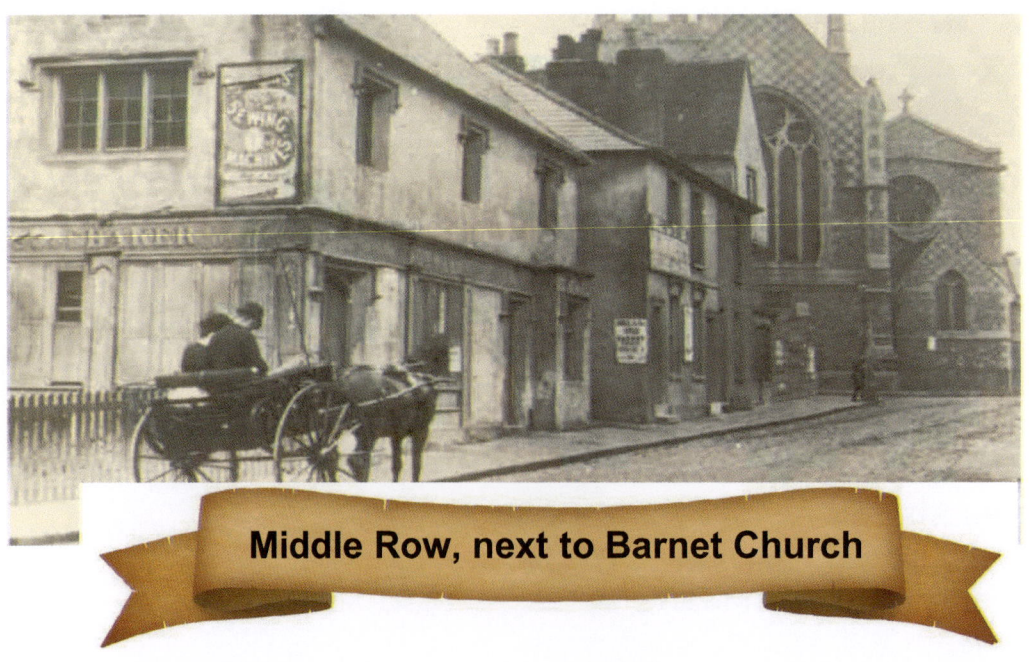

Middle Row, next to Barnet Church

Chipping Barnet was once the main coach stop during the days of horse drawn traffic and this part of Barnet has the majority of eating /drinking places and a wide selection of shops in the High Street, including the Spires.

And then along came the Railway (the mainline, New Barnet in 1850 and the suburban, High Barnet in 1872) and the town became less hectic as the horse had become a slow way of transport.

NEW BARNET.

If High and East Barnet have the history it was New Barnet that brought them both together when in 1850 the Great Northern Railway Company (GNR) took over the running of the railway line that avoided Barnet hill. They opened Barnet Station a mile and a half to the east of High Barnet and renamed it New Barnet in 1884. With the railways came the people and suddenly the population of Barnet rose as new houses were built for those that wanted to live away from the city. Main lines were not particularly intended for commuter travel, but the company soon realised their potential, and another station was opened on the edge of the expanding suburb of Oakleigh Park in 1873.

Privately run buses, transported people from the station and a newly built Station Road and a well-used footpath, the Meadway, were to become the route to High Barnet.

The age of the stage coach was over.

The Railway Bell was built not long after New Barnet station opened in 1850, as part of the general development of the area, and is now a Wetherspoon pub.

The original station booking office, mounted on the station bridge linking the platforms, was burnt down in a fire caused by a thunderstorm in August 1989. The station was refurbished shortly before this incident.

From 1894 New Barnet formed part of the East Barnet Urban District of Hertfordshire until 1965 when it was transferred from Hertfordshire to Greater London to become part of the newly-created London Borough of Barnet.

The former town hall still stands in Station Road. Local government use ended in the early 1990s and the property was sold off for use as a restaurant. In 2006 the building was converted into flats.
Today New Barnet has become the most populated area in Barnet with an abundance of flats in Station Road where once big houses (and churches) stood.

The main commercial area in New Barnet is on East Barnet Road, near the railway station. A number of office blocks were built in Station Road in the 1960s & 70s. Some have now been converted to flats. A large Sainsbury's supermarket (opened 30 September 1980) is surrounded by a cluster of small independent shops.

This is a picture of "Mallard" passing through New Barnet station which still holds the record speed (126 miles an hour in) for a steam train.
The station use to be a popular place for train spotters.

~ 11 ~

EAST BARNET

Although High Barnet has the history it is East Barnet that is the oldest Barnet.

Since the Norman Conquest, East Barnet has been part of the manor of Chipping Barnet. The church, St Mary the Virgin, consists of a nave, built by an Abbot of St Albans early in the 12th century.

A mill which is recorded as having belonged to the abbot of St. Albans in 1291) probably stood on Pymme's Brook, but there is no trace of one now.

Daniel Augustus Beaufort, the geographer, was born at East Barnet. The Royal Irish Academy owed its formation in great part to his exertions. His most important work was his map of Ireland, published in 1792, and accompanied by a memoir of the civil and ecclesiastical state of the country. He is also known for the prominent part he took in the foundation of Sunday schools, and in the preparation of elementary educational works.

East Barnet Fire Brigade 1903

East Barnet village has been there for years and many of the locals have seen the changes.

In the East Barnet Urban District (including New Barnet) 13,514 people lived there in 1921, 18,549 in 1931 and over 30,000 by 1939.

From 1894 until 1965 East Barnet formed part of the East Barnet Urban District of Hertfordshire. In 1965, it was transferred from Hertfordshire to Greater London and its former area was amalgamated with Barnet Urban District, Friern Barnet Urban District, Finchley Borough and Hendon Borough to form the new London Borough of Barnet.

The biggest park in town is Oakhill Park, which is the venue for the East Barnet Festival.

Walk the dog or watch a game of football, this park has it all with tennis courts and children's playground.

There is also supposed to be the ghost of a medieval knight who has appeared in full armour on horseback galloping across the park and an ancient oak tree burst into flames on a clear summer's day early in the 20th century.

There used to be a cinema where Budgens now stands and at this moment in time the Prince of Wales is the only pub in the village now that The Cat and Lantern and the Kings Head have closed down.

There are shops and restaurants that offer a choice of international foods.

It only takes a few minutes to walk through the village and it does have a car park.

HADLEY.

Hadley, or Monken Hadley, owes its name to "its elevated situation, Headleagh signifying in the Saxon "a high place" (To the west the land rises to 400 feet above sea level).
The manor belonged to the Mandevilles till the middle of the 12th century, when it was alienated by Geoffrey de Maneville to the Abbey of Walden, hence the designation Monken (or Monk's) Hadley.
History should have taught us about "The Battle of Hadley" but it is Barnet that is remembered when in fact the battle was fought up on Hadley Green.
Monken Hadley was originally a civil parish of Middlesex forming part of a small protrusion into Hertfordshire.
In 1889, under the Local Government Act 1888, the civil parish was transferred to Hertfordshire. Under the Local Government Act 1894 the parish was split with a Hadley parish becoming part of the Barnet Urban District, while the remaining part of the parish became part of the East Barnet Urban District of Hertfordshire.

In 1965, under the London Government Act 1963, its area was transferred to Greater London and combined with that of other districts formerly in Hertfordshire and Middlesex to form the present-day Barnet. There are some lovely houses in Hadley including the house that David Livingstone lived in and many are a good example of Georgian architecture.
It's a nice walk through Hadley that could end up in Hadley woods which is a must to visit. Find your way to Jacks Lake and you can walk the dog or just take an easy stroll past the fishermen that frequent the lake.

Its real name is Beech Hill Lake but it takes its present name from Charles Jack, owner of Beech Hill Park until his death in 1896, who was responsible for the building development at Hadley Wood.
There is also a fishing club here.

Rowing boats used to be available for hire and a Sunday walk to the woods via the Hadley Hotel was a weekly part of the early 20th century.

Hadley Common has a cricket field, home to a well-known cricket club, Monken Hadley CC, which is mentioned in one of the works of the author Anthony Trollope, who lived in Monken Hadley.
Other famous well know celebrities who were lucky enough to live in this beautiful part of North London were Lennox Lewis: World heavyweight boxing champion, Kingsley Amis who wrote the comedy book which became a film and a TV series "Lucky Jim" and probably one of the funniest comedians in the world Spike Milligan (who you can read about on page ??). Hadley also has a beautiful church (which you can read about on page 61. Many famous footballers live in this area.

Hadley church

BARNET HILL.

After Samuel Pepys paid one of his regular visits to Barnet Physic Well in 1660, he mentioned that the road thereto was *"only one path and torne, plowed, and digged up, owing to the waggoners carrying excessive weights of over one ton, with more than five horses and oxen to a team"*.

In 1754 a decision was made to construct a fair turnpike across Finchley Common but people so little understood the advantage of rendering the transit of goods easy that they obstructed the work. However, the responsibility of making good the highway was given to The Highgate and Whetstone Road Trust and by 1810 it was considered that the eight miles from London to Whetstone was one of the best roads in the kingdom.

In 1823 the then Trustees were informed that the improvement of the whole of The Great North Road from London to Holyhead had been put into the hands of Thomas Telford who declared that the mile and a bit between Pricklers Hill and Barnet town was in need of drastic improvement.
This came as a financial shock to the Trustees as they thought the main repairs would only apply to that part of the road passing through North Wales and not locally. They entrusted themselves to their own surveyor, James McAdam, to oversee the works.

The early 19th century road ran comparatively smoothly along the Whetstone ridge until its descent at Pricklers Hill by the county boundary. It sloped unevenly down, rising again at Underhill House [near where Western Parade is today]. Again it dropped to where Mays Lane curved away beyond the Old Red Lion and then it began its long ascent to the town of Barnet, following a line roughly parallel to Vale Drive before meeting the steepness of the escarpment. It joined the High Street at Victoria Lane, known then as Hog Lane, just below The Red Lion Hotel.

Teams of horses would be waiting at Underhill to be attached to coaches and carriers carts. Hauling was big business in those days for Barnet Hill was a challenge especially in poor weather.
Many times passengers had to alight and walk the hill if no extra pairs were available. Work on Pricklers Hill began and an embankment was raised to smooth out the slope towards Underhill.
This ridge is very evident from within Greenhill Park and from the houses on the eastern side. The stream which flowed from the Greenhill House lakes into Dollis Brook was diverted through a drain beneath the road.
Meanwhile Telford had plans for Barnet town. He suggested excavating a gorge through the hilltop in order to lower its brow, the spoil from which would be have been used to level out the severity of the escarpment. This would have the effect of leaving houses overlooking and possibly overhanging an ugly chasm.

John Loudon McAdam was a Scottish civil engineer and road-builder and he came up with an alternative suggestion being what we see today.
His plan was to remove a large quantity of earth from the adjoining fields belonging to the Corporation of the Sons of the Clergy, and for taking a portion of their land to raise an embankment a heavy compensation had to be paid by the Trust. In order to meet this expense it became necessary to borrow money by mortgaging the future tolls of the road. Work began in 1823 and the final cost, including interest, was expected to reach £17,000. It was clear that in order to meet this expense, and cover the upkeep of the road, the tolls were inadequate. They lobbied to obtain an additional Act which would empower them to increase the tolls, and here there was further pressure as the notorious Bill for the London and Birmingham Railway was also being applied for.
However, the Trustees obtained their Act of Parliament and raised the tolls such that a coach would have to pay more than three shillings [15p] to pass the tollgate. The tolls were let by auction at a sum of £7530 per annum (which equated to more than fifty thousand carriages) and the Trustees began to repay their debts.

By the 3rd February 1842 the last payment was made.
It has been said that old ploughshares, iron bedsteads and cannons captured in the Napoleonic War were sunk into the soil to hold it all together. Nevertheless, The Birmingham Railway Bill was passed and the rest is history.
Coach travel became obsolete as goods and passengers found they could traverse the countryside quicker by rail and the Whetstone tollgate was discarded in 1863.
Richard Selby

Buses stop near High Barnet tube station which is on Barnet Hill

At the top of Barnet Hill stands the church of ST JOHN THE BAPTIST which is known locally as

BARNET CHURCH.

There is evidence from the Manor Court records that there has been a place of worship on this site since the 13th century. By the early 15th century with the town growing fast and a bigger church was needed for the community. John de la Moote, the Abbot of St Albans, rebuilt the body of the church, which consisted of a Chancel, nave and aisles, separated by pointed arches rising from clustered columns, with a low embattled tower at the west end.

During the Reformation statues were damaged or destroyed, carvings smashed, windows broken and valuables stolen. However, after the succession of Queen Mary, a Roman Catholic, the Latin Mass was once again used in the church.

Under Queen Elizabeth's reign, records show that there were three hundred communicants in Chipping Barnet and in the reign of James 1st a vestry was added. By 1800, the Great North Road had become the major highway to the north and Barnet provided a convenient stopping place after leaving London.

In the early years of the 19th century the church was enlarged and it was completely restored by 1875. The galleries were removed completely; the old churchyard to the south was used for a new nave and tower and the old 1420 church incorporated into a double north aisle.

The tomb of Thomas Ravenscroft

A fire in 1974 severely damaged the choir vestry, then under the tower, and threatened to destroy the whole building. It was put out just in time, and in the aftermath, ideas came forward for some of the changes which were put into effect in 1984. These included new glass doors as the main entrance under the tower, the creation of a new choir vestry and alterations to the organ.

If you enter the main door there is a font in front of you. To the right is a door with a gold knob. It is said that the door knob is in line with the cross on the top of St Pauls Cathedral.
It is also said that the top of Barnet Church is the highest point to York in the North and the Ural mountains to the east.

This is a beautiful church and the view from the top of the building is as good as any you will get in London.
The tower is open for viewing in the summer. Contact the church for more details.

LONDONS MAIN COACHING STOP.

There have been many forms of transport coming and going to Barnet. The tube station is at the end of the Northern Line and the town is a terminal for buses that go all over London. It's not surprising that Barnet has so much traffic as years ago it was also busy. With the coming of the stage coach Barnet became one of the most important towns in the country with 150 horse drawn vehicles coming and going through the town every day.

The smell must have been awful but they probably had lovely roses!

The town was full of inns and taverns to cater for those coming into or going out of London and rouges and villains were in abundance, looking for a weakness in their wealthy prey.

With an eye to billeting, the War Office in 1756 compiled a national list of inns with beds and stabling in the town. There were 25 along Barnet Hill and High Street, ranging in size from the Green Man, with 18 beds and stabling for 31 horses, the Red Lion (15 beds/28 horses), and the Harts Horns (12 beds/50 horses), down to the Bulls Head and the Woolpack with one bed apiece and no stabling.

And then along came the Railway (the mainline in 1850 and the suburban in 1872) and the town became less hectic as the horse became a slow way of transport.

"TALLY-HO!" TO BARNET.
by Richard Selby

When Barnet was the gateway to the North, back in the 19th century, over 150 coaches would pass through the town every DAY. Here local historian and author Richard Selby takes you on a fictional coach journey to the top of the hill.

Rain spiked my face and blurred my vision and neither the brim of my hat nor the high collar of my cloaked coat kept it from running down my neck. I held on to a rail for dear life as the coach lurched and swayed over the rutted track and I took no solace that the other nine passengers perched perilously across the roof were just as miserable.

I bruised my back on the sharp corners of a trunk or one of the cases which shared the spine of the coach and I had to steady myself by locking my feet under other luggage which had been strapped to its sides. The coach was dreadfully over laden and perilously top heavy. My shoes had been soaked in soggy mud and I shivered in the dampness. The journey had been tiring, although we had been gone from Holborn for only two hours. An average of about five miles an hour was to be expected in those conditions and at least I was not walking to Barnet.

Some of the road users stepped aside into the bushes to avoid the mud which splashed around the horses' hoofs and from the great wheels. I looked past the driver and saw steam rise from the labouring animals. Their backs were a lustre of sweat and rain and their odour filled the air. We had not stopped at Whetstone for the gate had been opened when the keeper heard us coming. Our guard had sounded his distinctive tarantara when three furlongs distant which gave the gatekeeper at least two minutes to don his cloak. All of us apprentices recognised the particular calls of the coaches. The Mail Coaches horned authoritative fanfares for they had a time schedule to uphold.

Woe betides their drivers who let a precious minute be lost. We were only riding on a stage coach which would get to its destination when it could.

Water lay in dark pools and puddles for despite the road having been metalled with block some years previously ruts had been worn through the surface and were full of sludge. We never knew just how deep they were until the wheels sank to their axles. However, the coachman deliberately drove us through the well-worn tracks, for to miss a furrow would have meant that the coach would ride up on one side and probably upturn us. There were ladies trying to retain some modicum of modesty and bearing beside me.

They, likewise, had chosen to pay half fare for the topside ride. Those who could afford to ride inside, four men that day, were being thrown about a claustrophobic cabin. We considered ourselves lucky that we were the outsiders.

Despite the rain there was nothing as exhilarating as that kind of journey. Sometimes the coachman would let me take the reins, and that was a treat with all four horses responding to my left hand. My right held the whip and occasionally I used it to spur the charges ahead. But that day all I could think about was staying in my place.

The coach slowed to cross tracks as the bulk of a covered waggon appeared ahead. It too was making for Barnet but its journey was very slow. The waggoner walked beside its train guiding the leaders along the road. As we passed them I counted eight heavy horses linked in pairs struggling to grip the mud. Each step of their way was laboured as they sank to their fetlocks in the mud-filled ruts. They were caked in layers of filth and their burden seemed more than the load they hauled. The wagon probably carried a dozen tonnes and I wondered what it was that it transported. Could it have been building materials or foodstuffs? I let the thought fade as the coach returned to its original tracks with much rocking and noise. The springs holding the carriage above the axles were of leather and steel so they screeched loudly as they stretched to their limits. When another coach approached from the other direction we came to a halt and the coachmen exchanged tidings.

~ 23 ~

It was quite four minutes before ours was reminded of his purpose by a shout from within and we continued.

Each of us gave greetings to the passengers on the opposite vehicle with much hat touching and waving of hands. They were delighted to hear that Trafalgar had been won as we called the good news across the road.

The hamlet was before us but we had first to negotiate the decline of Pricklers Hill.

We passed Underhill House and descended again towards the cottages which lay below the next climb into Barnet. It would have been nightfall before we arrived but I held an introduction to a Mrs Scarbody who owned the Queens Head in Hadley. She would find me a bed for the night if I could afford no other, and I was ready for her hospitality. The coach rolled down into the yard of the Lower Red Lion where two of our passengers alighted. I helped to throw down their portmanteaux and other luggage.

The coachmen checked that an additional team was available and ostlers brought a pair from their stables already harnessed for attaching to our leaders. The guard shouted out a warning to us to hold on and the coach, now with six horses, was led out for the procession to Barnet.

The train was led by the ostler from the Red Lion riding astride the front pair and we proceeded at his pace, which in all honesty was not much slower than the journey we had so far endured. On my previous visit no spare teams had been available and the most nimble of the passengers had been made to walk the hill.

The incline steepened and the horses strained more than they had in the past ten miles. They had coped well with the climb to Islington and had overcome Highgate Hill without flagging. Their passage through Finchley Common had been a drag and I was full of admiration at this, their final challenge of the day. I wondered just how many teams would need to be linked to the wagon which we had passed fifteen minutes previously.

The hill took a few minutes to ascend but the lights of the town lay ahead of us, and I began to anticipate the hot meal and a glass or two of ale. The tower of the church was silhouetted against the last colours of the evening sky which had begun to show through the breaking clouds. Slowly, ever so slowly, our coach approached the houses, cottages and inns.

Most of their chimneys exuded smoke which hung in the damp, windless air. The rain had eased but the road remained slippery despite the surface of the hill having been prepared in a proper manner, and plentiful hay had been strewn to soak up the mud and manure.

Our way was blocked by a lone cow but the leadsman gave it a kick and it returned down a side alley.

The bulk of Middle Row divided the road as it widened. Inns and taverns, alehouses and shops were around us when we reached the brow of the hill and we stopped for the spare horses to be unhitched.

"To those who ride with us to Biggleswade," shouted the coachman, "be in the yard of the Boar's Head at seven of the clock. That is in one half hour, if you please."

I glanced at the clock on the church and wondered if it chimed the hours. Thankfully I was not to be continuing my journey until the morrow.

We dismounted and I watched to see where my fellow passengers retired. The gentlemen from within stretched their legs and walked into the Kings Head. Moments later liveried boys ran out to collect their luggage. I nodded farewell to my companions and stepped out on to the High Street as the coach was led through the arch of the Boar's Head. I looked around to recall my memories for it had been awhile since I had

ventured this way on my journeys home to the Midlands and I intended to spend the evening with acquaintances that I had met on an earlier visit. There was a pennant hanging bedraggled from the mast on the church tower. The stones in its graveyard stood worn and ready to fall, and the few that had toppled were already overgrown with the briars of neglect. The town was old and the houses were an assortment of design and purpose. Cooking pots within teased my nose with vapours which escaped through open windows. Alleyways seemed to tunnel themselves between the overhanging timbers of adjacent houses, down which I spied goats tethered amidst sleepy hens in the yards behind.

Hearty laughter turned my head to the open door of an ale-house through which I could see the flames of the hearth adding warmth to its patrons' fellowship. "It is good to be here again,"
I remember saying to myself with an air of blissful recollection, and in heady anticipation stepped out towards Hadley.

Richard Selby wrote the popular "Barnet Pubs Another Round"

The foregoing account is an imaginary journey to Barnet at the start of the nineteenth century. However it would indeed have been as romantic, for the details are correct as far as records tell us.

Barnet Hill was not an easy route to travel until it was straightened and smoothed out in the 1820's, but it lay on the Great North Road and just before the divide of the roads at Hadley.

The town was a staging point where the horses were changed; a place where passengers could alight, rest and take refreshment in their journey north, or freshen up before the final stage into London. Barnet abounded with establishments solely for the replenishment of man and beast.

How travellers would dine at a coaching inn

BARNET PUBS.

"Oliver limped slowly into the little town of Barnet, wondering at the great number of public houses-every other house in Barnet was a tavern large or small"

Oliver Twist: Chapter 8 by Charles Dickens

There was always an abundance of public houses in Barnet helped by the fact that the town was an important coaching stop. According to Richard Selbys excellent book "Barnet Pubs" there have been over 200 places of liquid refreshment in Barnet. We even had our own brewery in Hadley.
Many of the pubs are now disappearing and over a dozen have closed in the last 30 years.

From the far end of Barnet High Street down to East Barnet Village there were many pubs that served the people of Barnet. Since medieval times inns and taverns have supplied the local residents with a wide variety of liquid refreshment and a meeting place where talk is of every subject under the sun.

Some have kept the same name for years but others changed the sign outside and there has been drinking establishments since the "Swan on the Hoop" opened at 46-50 Barnet High Street, between the Mitre and Park Road, way back in 1398.

There have been over twenty pubs opened from the Meadway to the Barnet Church where now only the Kings Head, the Red Lion and the Mitre stand.

But the pub is still an important part of any community and Barnet has a wide selection to attract customers in a variety of ways. It may be sport on TV, Quiz nights, live music or simply a nice atmosphere.
It is a place where people from different walks of life can meet to chat or eat and over the past few years they have made women feel at ease in what was once a male dominated domain.

The snug and the public bar have gone and crisps and peanuts are replaced by real ale pie and chicken and chips.

The majority of Barnet pubs have remained unchanged over the past 50 years and each have their locals who have probably been drinking in the same pub for years so nothing has changed that much since the 14th century.

According to Richard Selby the Kings Head (1626) is the oldest pub and the Mitre (1633) the oldest inn.

BYGONE PUBS IN BARNET.

If you want to know about Barnet public houses, inns or taverns past and present there is no other way than to read the excellent "Barnet Pubs – Another Round" By Local historian Richard Selby.

Within the past few years our local pubs have been closed down and they become a part of the history of Barnet. Many of us remember the local that is no longer there and here are a few that have gone to that big brewery in the sky! We hope they bring back a few memories of good times spent (and good money!)
If we work our way from Hadley down to New Barnet there are 7 pubs that have disappeared.

**THE TWO BREWERS:
1726 – 1990.**
A nice pub where you could take the children to play in the garden. Bad news it was a Watneys pub. Now Houses.

KING WILLIAM IV:
1727 - 2004 Listed Building.
Popular with the locals of Hadley it had low ceilings and an old world charm. Was a fish restaurant.

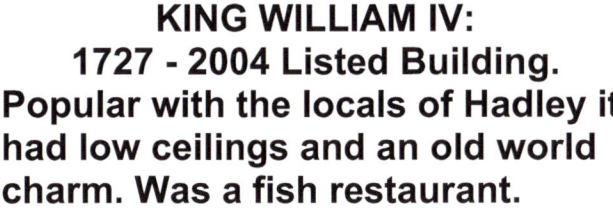

THE WINDMILL: 1756 - 1999.
The pub commemorated the windmill that use to stand a few yards across the road. There used to be tea gardens there and it was popular with people going to Hadley Woods.

THE GREEN MAN: 1691 - 2007.
One of the old pubs of Barnet. Trade really took off when they built the St Albans Road. Became popular in recent years as being one of the music pubs in Barnet.

THE SALISBURY: 1839 – 1988.
Another popular pub with the locals. Had Trad Jazz on Sunday mornings and was demolished in 1988. It is now the site of Iceland. The sign is in the Barnet Museum.

THE CROWN AND ANCHOR: 1852 - 2005
Also known as The Boars Head and the Saracens Head. It was there one day and gone the next. Could have become a good music venue.

THE DUKE OF LANCASTER: 1868 – 2000.
Now this was a good music venue, probably the best Barnet has had. Many top bands played here in the 70s. Sadly missed.

THE ALBION: 1836 – 2008.
Another popular watering hole that was known for a nice pint of Abbots. Mainly used by locals the Albion will be remembered by many.

THE LYTTON ARMS: 1872 – 1996.
Named after Edward Bulwer-Lytton Who wrote a novel about The Battle of Barnet in "The Last of the Barons".
The pub was popular for many years under the management of Greg and Lil and later by Keiren and Nora who went on to run the Railway Tavern.

THE WARWICK/ BAILEYS/THE BELL AND BUCK/.1869 -1998.
This a very good music pub but for some reason it was never capitalised on. Many will remember when it was called the Warick and the tales of that era.

THE ALEXANDRA. 1867 - 2015
East Barnet Road, Dating from the mid nineteenth century it was formerly known as the Alexandra Tavern and appears in newspapers under that name as early as 1869. It was probably built during the development of the area after the opening of nearby New Barnet railway station in 1850 It was on the corner with Victoria Road.
The pub was demolished in 2015 and replaced with housing.

THE WINE BAR /THE CAT AND LANTERN.
1987 - 2007

In the mid seventies the wine bar was the place to go if you liked real ale. Tim Martin (Weatherspoons) used to frequent it and there were just a few tables and benches but it became a fashionable meeting place. The owner changed the name to The Cat and Lantern and it becamea popular music venue.

THE OLD RED LION. 1750 – 2015.

Was the nearest pub to where Barnet FC used to play and a roll down the hill from High Barnet tube.
On 19th of February 2015 McMullens announced that they have sold the pub and it ceased trading a week later. An Asset of community was applied for but refused.
In 1986 it was listed by Barnet Council as being a building of local architectural or historic significance. Once again Barnet council failed to support and with Barnet F.C leaving for another borough the old Red Lion lost a lot of its trade.

THE WHITE LION 1839 – 2017.

The White Lion served its last customers on Sunday 12 March 2017. Many of the pub's regulars had met the previous evening for a farewell round of drinks. The White Lion opened in 1839 and was on the route of what was then Telford's famous road from London to Holyhead.

Alexandra Wood Street. 1867 – 2011. Some said the pub was haunted (Probably the spirits). It had a lovely garden that was popular in the summer.

Closed down in 2011, and is now a dwelling now a dwelling.

KINGS HEAD/THE DRUM.1715 – 2006.

The Drum was situated on Cat Hill. Previously known as The Kings Head and had been on site this since at least the mid-18th. It was known locally as The Drum and the name changed to that. The pub closed in 2006 and became a vets practice.

THE JESTER 1958
The Jester was situated at Mount Pleasant. NEAR Cockfosters. Built in 1958, the pub was listed as one of Camra's London Real Heritage Pubs. It closed in 2013 but in March 2018, the building caught fire, causing widespread damage as well as a roof collapse.

JUG & TRUMPET /BAR TEN/ EXCALIBUR/AFTER OFFICE HOURS.1991 – 2003
Situated next to the Bull theatre this site had many changes in names and it was a shame as After Office Hours was a good music venue.

All gone but not forgotten.

TUDOR HALL.

Next to Barnet College in Wood Street. This hall was built in 1577 and was used as Queen Elizabeth's Grammar School for Boys. It is the oldest known building in Chipping Barnet today.

Beneath the shadow of Barnet church this building has much of the Tudor style of architecture.

The school was founded in 1573 by Queen 1st, petitioned by Robert Dudley, Earl of Leicester, The charter for the school was granted *"at the humble request of our well-beloved cousin and counsellor, Robert Earle of Leicester, knight of the most noble Order of the Garter, Master of our house"*

Very few records of the history of the school exist although it is known that two of its early masters became bishop in Ireland and that one of its governors was imprisoned in the Tower of London.

The Statutes compiled for regulating the school in 1634 decreed that *"the master shall be a clergyman, approved by the Bishop of London, and that the scholars be male children, free from infectious disease; that the children of the residents in the parish of Barnet shall pay twenty shillings a year, and no more, but that for others a charge may be made, as the parents and master may agree"*.

The school contained over a hundred boys and it was repaired in 1597 and again in 1637. At one stage it became a private boarding school and it closed down in 1872 only to be restored in 1874 with many additions.

As the number of pupils outgrew the capacity of Tudor Hall, so the school was transferred in 1932 to a new site in Queen's Road, which backed on to the Stapylton field.

It was administered by the South Herts Division of Hertfordshire County Council, until 1965 when it became part of the borough of Barnet. In the 1960s, there were around 550 boys with 150 in the sixth form. Tudor Hall was completely restored in 1968 by the London Borough of Barnet, and is now part of Barnet College, although nobody seems to know why it is not part of the museum.

BARNET MUSEUM.
31 Wood Street, Barnet, Herts. EN5 4BE

Barnet Museum was opened in March 1938 at 31 Wood Street, to house the collection of the Barnet & District Local History Society. Its building is an attractive early Georgian house and the Museum contains archives, objects, prints, photographs, paintings and maps reflecting the development of Chipping Barnet and the surrounding area, as well as a notable collection of period costumes and accessories, domestic items and lace.

In addition to the town of Chipping Barnet the museum covers other nearby areas.

One of these is East Barnet, which formed part of the original manor of Chipping and East Barnet it is the latter that appears to have been the focus of the earliest settlement. The parish church of St Mary the Virgin, East Barnet dates from the first half of the eleventh century, whilst the church of St John the Baptist in Chipping Barnet dates from around 1250.

The town of New Barnet was created following the coming of the Great Northern Railway in 1850. Other areas that are covered by the Museum include West Barnet, Cockfosters, Arkley, Hadley, Whetstone and Totteridge. The Museum building is owned and maintained by the Borough, whilst the collection belongs to the Barnet & District Local History Society, whose members run the Museum itself.

Opening Hours Tuesday to Thursday 2.30pm – 4.30pm
Saturday 10.30am – 12.30pm & 2.00pm – 4.00pm   Sunday, Monday & Friday Closed

Visit their Web Site: http://www.barnetmuseum.co.uk

CYRIL FRISBY.

If you walk down Station Road New Barnet you might notice this plaque on the ground just before Plantagenet Road. This is dedicated to captain Cyril Frisby who was an English recipient of the Victoria Cross the highest and most prestigious award for gallantry in the face of the enemy that can be awarded to British and Commonwealth forces. He was awarded the VC for his actions in the Battle of Canal du Nord during the First World War.

He was born on 17 September 1885 in New Barnet, Frisby joined the Hampshire Regiment as a private in October 1916 and within weeks was undergoing officer training. He was commissioned in the Coldstream Guards in March 1917 as a second lieutenant. He was posted to the Western Front in November, where he joined the regiment's 1st Battalion. Early the following year, he was promoted to acting captain.

On 27 September 1918, during the Hundred Days Offensive, the Coldstream Guards was engaged in the Battle of Canal du Nord, near Graincourt. His battalion was tasked with the capture of a canal crossing, with Frisby himself in command of one of the attacking companies. Once over the canal, he was to set up defensive positions and make contact with the adjacent 3rd Guards Battalion. On reaching the canal, barbed wire, together with heavy fire from a German machine-gun post under the bridge on the far side of the canal halted the advance. Frisby, together with a lance-corporal, Thomas Jackson, and two others, got through the wire and climbed down into the canal under intense fire. With a further twelve men joining him, he led the capture of the post. Despite a leg wound, he then attended forming a defensive line as per his instructions. While doing so, he had led an adjacent leaderless company in fighting off a counter-attack.[3]
After the war Frisby spent much of his time tuna fishing, becoming prominent in the sport and competing in international fishing competitions. Frisby died on 10 September 1961 at his home in Guildford aged 75.

THE BATTLE OF BARNET.

(The story so far)

On Saturday 13th April 1471 thousands of men of the Lancastrian army marched into Barnet via Kitts End Lane (This was the old Holyhead/St Albans Road).They halted at Gladsmuir Heath, (now known as Hadley common), near the hamlet of Monken Hadley, just north of Barnet. The House of Lancaster were at war with the house of York who both thought that they had the right to rule England. It was the Red Rose of the Lancastrians backing Henry VI (who was a prisoner of Edward) against the White Rose of the Yorkists who thought that Edward IV should be the rightful heir to the throne.

The war of the Roses had started in 1455 with The Battle of St Albans and for 16 years both sides fought out many battles but this one was to have consequences that would affect English history.

Leading the Lancastrians was Richard Neville, Earl of Warwick, more commonly known as "The King Maker". Neville had once been a good friend and advisor to Edward, the man he was about to face on the battlefield.

EDWARD IV

WARWICK
The kingmaker

~ 38 ~

That Saturday the Kingmaker and his advisors probably spent the day choosing a good position for the forth coming battle. As Barnet is on a plateau he had the advantage of the high ground would put the Lancastrians in a favourable position wait for Edward to come out of London.

It is here that we should point out that the Barnet Tourist Board believes that there is a possibility that past accounts of the formation of the two sides could be mistaken by historians.

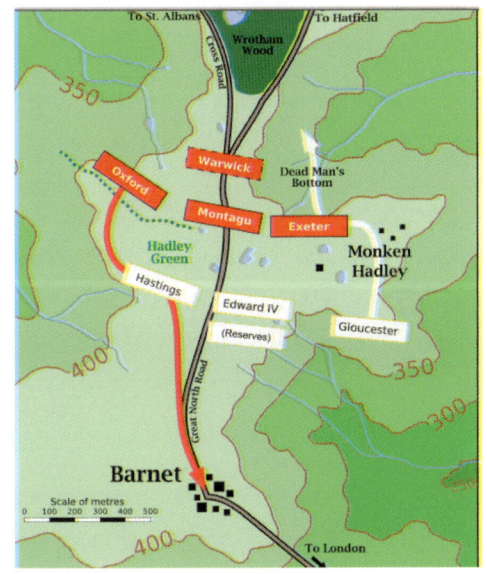

Most relate that the battle formation was like this:

But we believe that it could have been this:

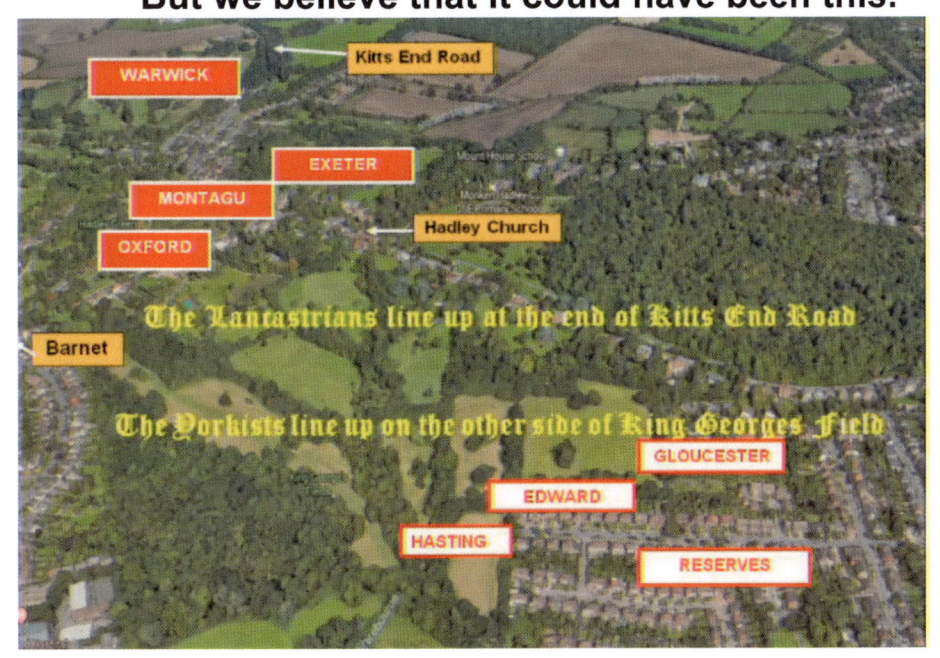

The Lancastrians line up at the end of Kitts End Road

The Yorkists line up on the other side of King Georges Field

(If you want to find out more about our theory you can read another of our publications "The search of the battlefield" available on Amazon)

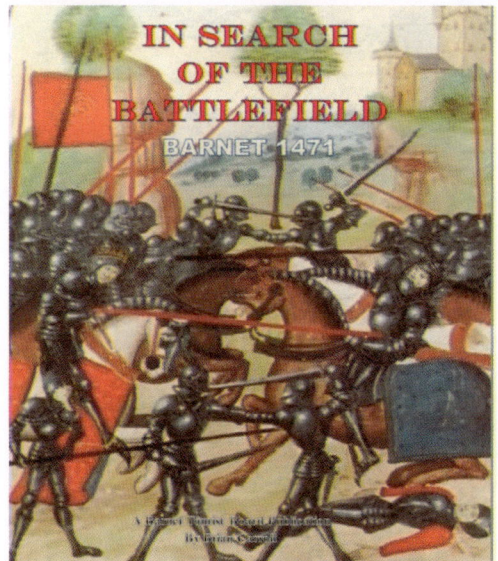

The road through Barnet was a traveller's road and there were six ale houses to cater for them. That day Edward probably made one of his wisest decisions when, with over 10,000 men, thirsty from all the work they had done, gave the order not to stop in the town but to line up on the other side, on the edge of Hadley Common.

Whether that decision was made because he did not want to let his men loose in the town or that he wanted them to have a clear head for the fight in the morning, it was the right one. As night fell Edward ordered his troops to silence as the enemy were no more than a quarter of a mile up the road.
In the dark King Edward's troops were not lined up directly opposite the Lancastrians and this was to be an important part of the battle.
It was dark and the two sides were about five minutes away from each other as they settled down for the night, waiting for the morning and the fight that was to come.
Take a walk up Barnet High Street today, and when you reach the edge of Hadley Common it is quite easy to imagine the area when it was flat, with no houses or buildings in the way. If you stand at the southern end of the common, where Edward drew up his forces, you cannot see the Hadley monument which is roughly where Warwick drew up his forces and yet nearly 20,000 men were due to fight in this small area. As neither side seemed to have an idea of the position of the other on the field, it is hard to imagine how two forces of so many men could not hear each other, even if visibility was nil in the total darkness.

EASTER SUNDAY 14th April 1471 between 4.am and 5.am.

The sun rose over Barnet and both sides were ready for battle. At the rear Henry, The deposed king who Edward had brought along, was being well guarded, meaning that Barnet can boast three kings of England who stayed there that night, (the Duke of Gloucester later became Richard III).

On that spring day the common was covered by a thick mist and the gunfire from the Lancastrians the previous night did little to help visibility as both sides waited until it was clear enough to start the battle. It was Edward who led the attack after he ordered no quarter, and it probably took a couple of minutes for the enemy to come face to face, swinging axes, swords and pikes at anything that appeared before them. There is not enough space here to cover the whole of the battle (see "The Battle of Barnet" @ www.barnet4u.co.uk) that took place just outside our town and it was voted in the top 10 of the most important battles in English history and it paved the way for the end of the Plantagenets and the beginning of a new royal household, The Tudors.

Mistakes by both sides and cries of "Treachery" led to the Lancastrians fleeing the battlefield and Edward becoming the Victor and the King of England.

Warwick was slain near the site of the monument at Hadley and with his death went the last real hope of the Lancastrians regaining the throne. It did not last long, perhaps four or five hours, and it was not the bloodiest. But the list of casualties was like no other before or after it and over 10, 000 arrows were apparently collected on the field afterwards.

If the Battle had happened in America there would probably be a monument or tee shirts for sale but our council and our heritage organisations have done nothing to commemorate an important part of English history except a monument that could be in the wrong place and not really highlighted.

Perhaps we can teach more about the battle in our local schools and the Barnet Tourist Board is looking into this.

We also have a mystery on our doorstep in that after the battle there were thousands of bodies lying on the common. We know that villagers from around Barnet came and buried the bodies in two mass graves but no one has ever found them.

The location of the actual battlefield is in dispute and until the day definite proof of where the battle took place is known we can only go on the history books that put the site as being just north of the Monk (The public house). The facts about the battle and its outcome remain the same.

WHERE ARE THE BODIES BURIED?

On Easter Sunday 14th April 1471 the armies of the house of Lancaster and the house of York faced each other on the outskirts of Barnet in what was to be one of the decisive battles in the war of the roses. Within five hours the white rose of York had defeated the red rose of Lancaster and thousands of bodies lay scattered on Hadley common.

This battlefield, around Hadley Green, was voted in the top 10 battles in history establishing itself among the likes of The Somme in France and Little Bighorn in Montana, USA, in a list compiled by experts writing for the Sunday Times Travel section.

Clearing the battlefield would have got underway quickly in view of the warm weather, and most of the dead were probably buried within a week. The carnage on the field would have been a truly appalling sight. Estimates of the number killed vary greatly, as with most 15th Century battles, but it is likely to have been between 2,000 and 3,000 although some have put it as high as 10,000.

10,000 arrows were apparently collected on the field afterwards and artillery would have been left where it was abandoned. Bodies with limbs hanging off and the sound of men screaming in pain would have filled the air in Barnet. Thousands of pints of blood flowed in the ponds and the fields of the small area that the main battle took place.

Most of the tales of the Battle of Barnet state that the bodies were buried in a place called "Deadman's bottom" It has also been mentioned that Lancastrian solders ran into "Deadman's" and were slaughtered. Some put the "the bottom" as being here on the Potters Bar road opposite Wrotham Park. Other stories say that it is in the top end of Hadley wood Most of the dead were buried in grave pits on the field as the black plague was still fresh in some people minds.

The locals would have been aware that they had to clean up and be quick. Most of the bodies would have been stripped of armour and anything valuable by the Yorkists who were drifting back to London. Some of those of noble birth would be taken away to be buried with more dignity in family tombs.

There is a story that Edward paid for a chapel to be built near the site of the battle where prayers were said for those who died.

Although the Lancastrians lost heavyweights such as Warwick and Montagu, the Yorkists, lost far more noblemen than they had in any other battle. It is said that the chapel was built either above or near to the grave pits. The exact position was never recorded, but it was mentioned during the following century in the St. Albans Abbey records, concerning repairs and maintenance. After the Reformation, the chapel was abandoned and nothing was heard about it again.

Part of it is supposed to be incorporated in Pimlico House, which lies beside the common"

Somewhere close to the Hadley Highstone the answer could be found. How long would it take to remove all the bodies? In what were they transported? Did they burn the bodies and is there is no grave or pit? Did the people of Barnet come out after the battle and start right away? Who would organise such a task and how did they know where it was a safe distance to leave the bodies? Where would the ground be soft enough to dig (apparently) two large graves, one for either red or white rose follower? Is there anything to say that the bodies are buried somewhere in Hadley Woods or is it in some spot that nobody has yet thought of! Why, with so much building going on in Barnet has nothing ever been found? The clues are there but who has the answer?

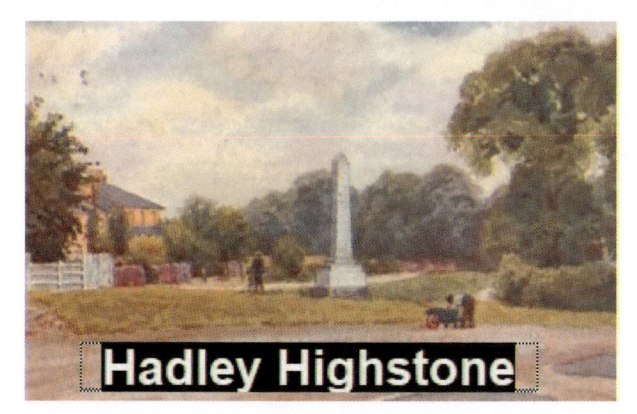

Hadley Highstone

WOULD THE BATTLE MAKE A GOOD FILM?

If you have seen movies such as "Brave Heart" you will know that a good battle scene is half of the story. The rest is a tale that can keep the audiences attention and so we all learned about William Wallace.

But would the story of "The Battle of Barnet" make an even better film as it has intrigue, love, betrayal and of course one of the most history changing battles in English history. It even has a tale of sorcery.

It's a story of two very good friends, Richard Neville, Earl of Warwick, (known as the Kingmaker) and the King of England Edward IV. In 1471 England had two kings fighting for the throne. Henry VI of the house of Lancaster, who had inherited the throne as an infant, and Edward IV of the house of York, who had seized the throne, and held Henry prisoner. They each had a son, (both called Edward), who had an equal right to become the future king. This was because both houses had descended from the same king, (Edward III) and the house of Plantagenet.

Neville was the second richest man in England (only the king had more wealth) and with his riches he had helped Edward to depose Henry and take the throne. Warwick was soon advising the young Edward and they had a close relationship during the early years of his reign. And then along came a woman.

Her name was Elizabeth Woodville and she eventually turned her husband against his old friend.

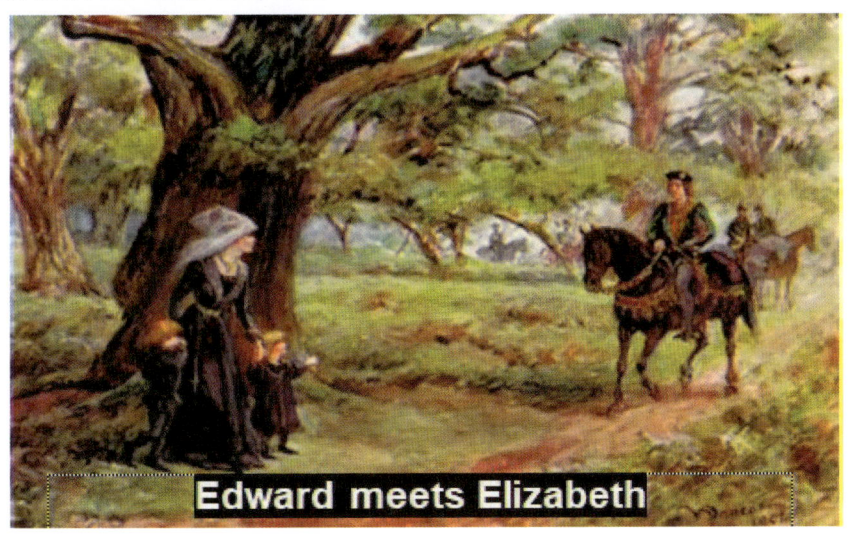

Edward meets Elizabeth

But Warwick was a shrewd and devious man, and he had another plan to make himself more powerful.

Edward's younger brother George, Duke of Clarence, was jealous of the king and in 1469 he married Warwick's eldest daughter Isabel.

The Duke now had a chance to be "The Kingmaker" if he could get Clarence onto the throne. With this in mind they raised an army against the king, which ended in defeat. They both headed for what they saw as the safety of France.

The king declared Warwick and Clarence traitors, and once more Edward was in control of the country.

Warwick was never short of ideas. He realised that his route to the throne by Clarence stood little chance, so another daughter would be used as a pawn. King Henry's wife, Queen Margaret, and the young Prince of Wales were also in exile in France. She hated Warwick as it was he who had taken the crown from her husband, who was still imprisoned in the Tower of London. The Lancastrians had been in exile for many years and were impatient to get home to see their families. Eventually she allowed Warwick to see her and he begged her forgiveness.

This she finally accepted. She also accepted Warwick's suggestion that his youngest daughter, Anne, become betrothed to Edward Prince of Wales which they did in July 1470. Once more Warwick had the chance to influence the future king and be "Kingmaker"

The Lancastrians planned their invasion of England and by September 1470 they were ready. They landed a force in southern England and headed inland, gathering more troops on the way. Edward was taken unawares, he was fighting in the North, and when he heard of Warwick's return he headed for London. But at Doncaster he was told that a large part of his army, led by The Marquis of Montagu, (Warwick's brother), had changed sides and would now be fighting against him. Trapped, and without enough men to win a battle,

Edward and his brother Richard Duke of Gloucester, (later to be crowned Richard III) decided it was better to run and fight another day so they made for Bruges and his old friend Louis de la Gruthuse, the Governor of Holland.

With Edward no longer in the country the land was in chaos. Order had to be restored. Warwick did this by putting Henry back on the throne, but at his coronation it was noticed that many of the Lords and knights present wore the bear and ragged staff badge of Warwick. Once the old king was dead the Earls daughter would be queen, and he would again be a leading figure at court.

King Edward had wasted no time in building an invasion army during his absence and by early March 1471 he had enough men to set sail for his homeland and landed at the Humber on the 14th March. With their large force they marched into London and Henry VI was once again made prisoner in the Tower of London.

Warwick marched south, with a large and well provisioned artillery train, and on Good Friday April 12th 1471 his Lancastrian army marched to St Albans, and camped on the outskirts. The next day he led his army into Barnet to wait for the army of Edward to come out of London. The young king took up the challenge and taking Henry with him he led his army to the outskirts of the capital.

That night there would be 3 kings sleeping in the town as Edwards's brother the Duke of Gloucester who would play an important part of the battle would later become Richard the third.

On Easter Sunday April 14th 1471. The fog hung over the common, help by the smoke from the artillery that had been going on the night before.

At 5 am Edward attacked, knowing that his old friend was less than half a mile down the road ready to face him in battle.

Edward ordered no quarter which meant that his friendship meant no more. It is said that the order was miss heard and that he wanted Warwick to be captured alive but in the battle that followed it was every man for himself and chivalry was casted aside.

The battle was ferocious as sword, lances and battle-axes were used with a means of survival.

The battle lined up with Warwick to the north behind his main force in reserve with the horses. When both side lined up to face each other the night before they were not allied and when the morning came the right hand side of Edwards army was over lapping Warwick's left.
This also meant that Lord Oxford on Warwick's right overlapped Edward VI on his left. As the two armies attacked each other oxford attacked the left hand side of the king's army and chased them into the town of Barnet.
Whether they stayed and had a drink or two is not recorded but by the time they got back to the battle the line of the fight had changed.
When Oxford rode back to the battle he came upon his own army but thought it was the enemy and attacked.
The cry of treachery went up and in the confusion The Lancastrians fled the field and it was victory for Edward and The Yorkists.

The Kingmaker is killed

As victory was in sight Edward learnt about the order of no quarter and gave a new order that Warwick was to be brought before him alive.

Unfortunately in the heat of the battle this order never got through and Knights cornered Warwick and killed him, apparently they stabbed him in the eyes. It was one of the bloodiest battles in English history and there could be up to 10,000 bodies buried on the unfound site.
It was the white rose of the house of York that won that day and Edward and Elizabeth kept the Lancastrians in power until the defeat of Richard III at the battle of Bosworth when the house of Plantagenet would give way to the Tudors.
The Lancastrians had been defeated and with the death of Warwick the kingmaker he would take no more part in deciding English history as it was a woman who won the kings heart.

BARNET MARKET

On August 23rd 1199 King John granted the abbot of St Albans the right to hold a weekly market every Thursday in Barnet. Many markets were founded around this time and those like Barnet with good locations brought profit both to the lord of the manor and to local inhabitants. The market gave Chipping Barnet its name and its urban character:

The original market place was at the top of the hill, where the road junction also provided a conveniently wide area, even larger before the church was added, probably in the 13th century.

Other buildings, permanent stalls and eventually the market hall began to cluster against the church, forming a Middle Row with narrow streets either side. Middle Row was demolished in 1889. The market day was changed to Monday in 1588 and then to Wednesday, probably in the mid-18th century. In the mid-19th century the site was moved off the main road and into a space adjoining St Albans Road, and an extra market day, Saturday, was added in 1960.

Local people came to buy and sell food and pottery, but the market was also one of the major trading centres ringing London, selling cattle and livestock, wool and hides, corn and other grain, in quantities far beyond local needs. Here country drovers and carters sold their stock on to London dealers, and although some animals were driven on, others were fattened up and slaughtered by local butchers. In 1588 Queen Elizabeth I granted a new charter renewing the market and adding an annual fair. From the mid-19th century to the mid-20th the market was more exclusively concerned with cattle than previously and this may explain the success of a supplemental market at Mary Payne's Place, on the opposite, eastern, side of the High Street just north of Bath Place, specialising in fruit, vegetables and flowers brought in from the surrounding countryside. Also known as the Poor Man's Market, this too operated on a Wednesday, but also on Saturdays when it stayed open until 11 in the evening, allowing men who were still able to do so to collect provisions for Sunday lunch.It may have been started by ex-servicemen after World War I, and closed either in 1929, when John Swain's wanted to expand over the site, or within the following decade.

By 1850, the market had expired, killed off not only by Smithfield Market but also by the increase in coach traffic. Ironically, though, just at the point when we know that coaches had killed the market, the railways killed off coaching.

Coaches rapidly vanished, and drovers, animals and markets reclaimed the streets, although the hygienic disadvantages of a town-centre location remained obvious. By the mid-1860s the market was in Market Place next to the Green Man at the junction of St Albans Road.
The present market site, almost next door, came into operation in 1874 and until the 1940s there was a cattle market there.
Increased regulation of slaughtering meant that butchers preferred to buy ready processed meat from wholesalers and with fewer local farms it helped to hasten its decline, and the last cattle auction was held on 19 August 1959. The gates to the cattle pens and the weighbridge were sold, and the cleared site became a general, and still flourishing, stall market.

In November 1902 Crawter & Lawrence of Cheshunt purchased the Cattle Market following the death of Marchant Harland. John Harding Young, articled pupil to John Crawter and aged only 18 took over running it.

On 28th April 1910, John Harding Young himself purchased the Cattle Market (and continued the trading of Harland & Sons Estate Agents).

In 1932 John Harding Young's son, William (aka Bill Young), joined the business. Bill Harding Young is a name held in great affection by many people who still live in Barnet. Bill, an estate agent and qualified auctioneer, was utterly dedicated to Barnet Cattle Market and was instrumental in its success over many decades. Bill auctioned thousands of beasts from the St. Albans Road site. By 1949 the Cattle Market had started to decline and Bill Young began to auction other goods as well as livestock. Second-hand furniture was very popular.

On 19th August 1959 the final livestock auction took place in Barnet Cattle Market (it is believed that a black and white film of the last day may survive). Bill Young turned the area into a stall market and on August 22nd there were 25 stalls. Later it was not unusual to see 50 or more stalls. Barnet Market Ltd was formed.

In January 1999 Bill Young sold the site to Nigel and Melanie Walsh, the highest bidders in a sealed bidding sale. He included in the sale a clause that required that the site must remain a stall market for 15 years. Mr. and Mrs. Walsh stated at the time that they had no plans to redevelop the site. The 15-year clause ran out in 2014. However, in November 2005 planning consent was granted to Mr and Mrs Walsh for redevelopment of the St. Albans Road site. Consent stipulated that the site must continue in use as a stall market at ground floor level but could have 14 flats above. A basement car park for 27 cars would be required.

In January 2008 Barnet Market moved to a temporary site on Stapylton Road car park to enable the St. Albans Road scheme to be built.

The St. Albans Road site was cleared of all the old Cattle Market buildings, but the planned development never happened due to lack of finance.

The Market returned to the St Albans Road site in November 2009 which by then had a poor uneven surface and was surrounded by a dismal hoarding. Finally Mr and Mrs Walsh sold the site to UBS (the Swiss bank that, at the time, owned The Spires shopping centre) in December 2011. UBS stated that they would resurface the Market's site and plans were prepared.

However, UBS had their own financial issues which led them to sell both The Spires and the market site to the William Pears Group in May 2013. The William Pears Group decided that it was a high priority to improve the St Albans Road site and they pressed ahead with the plans that were originally commissioned by UBS. However, they had to obtain planning consent for the changes, which included a change of use such that the site could be used as a car park on non-market days.

Once this was obtained, work started quickly and the Market was moved to the bandstand area outside Waitrose for 5 weeks. Saunders Markets Ltd were contracted to run the Market and they took over for the first day back on the refurbished site which was Saturday, 9th November 2013.

There was no official opening ceremony, but Theresa Villiers MP did attend and made a short speech expressing appreciation for the efforts of all those who had helped to bring about the improvements. She, herself, had campaigned over a long period for the site improvements.

Since Mr and Mrs Walsh sold the market site in 2011, the Market has been tied to The Spires and its changes of owner. In 2015, the William Pears Group sold The Spires and with it, the market site, to AIMCO, a Canadian pensions company. AIMCO have employed Hunters Real Estate Investment Managers for the strategic management of their investment, while Savills are responsible for the day-to-day management. After considering their options, the Market's St Albans Road site has been sold by the owners for the construction of a Premier Inn. Once again, the Market has moved, this time the short distance to the bandstand area between Waitrose and Stapylton Road, where it is more visible.

Barnet Market today

Barnet Market now have their own web site with more history and an update on what is happening to the market.

Go to https://fobm.co.uk/

BARNET FAIR

On 6th February 1588 Queen Elizabeth I granted a charter to the Lord of the Manor of Barnet (Charles Butler and "his heirs and assigns") the right to hold a weekly market on Mondays and a twice yearly fair.

The reason for the fairs was a way of bringing people together and of course by bringing a large number of people in one place there were criminals on the prowl who would steal and drunks and fights were common. All fines for these offences were paid to the Lord of the Manor so he probably looked forward to the twice yearly events. Over the years Barnet fair became popular as unlike the present fair it was becoming famous as the place to go for livestock, especially horses and cattle.

In 1758 John Tomlinson, The Lord of the Manor of Barnet was granted permission to change the dates of the fairs from June to April for the first one and from October to September for the second due to it being better for business.

Animals were driven from all over the country to the Barnet fairs, with Cattle from Scotland, cows from Devon and ponies from Wales. The September cattle fair was held in fields near Wood Street (until 1909) and various fields around the town were used for herding and displaying the livestock.

In September 1834 it was reported in The Times that Barnet Fair was the largest cattle market in all of England with up to 40,000 animals on offer and £100,000 being taken in trade on the first day.

By the mid-18th century Barnet fair had become associated with horse racing and races were held on the last three days of the event. The course they ran on was where the present high Barnet station now is and the last race held there was "The Barnet Stakes" on September 6th 1870. But the fair carried on and the animals kept coming, usually to the land opposite High Barnet station.

By becoming more popular and with large amounts of money available crime became on the increase and in 1874 The Barnet Press reported that 20 plain clothes detectives, 4 sergeants and 44 policemen from London were brought in to be on duty at the fair. This probably did not work very well as in 1888 there was a serious attempt to close down the fair on the grounds that it had become a nuisance but local businessmen got together a petition that stated " *It has been ascertained that an average of over 20,000 persons attend Barnet on each fair day and expenditure in the town and neighbourhood alone is estimated at upwards from £10,000 to 312,000 among tradesmen and farmers*"

This was only from the September fair as the April one had ended in 1881 when the area around Wood Street became part of Barnet common. The Home secretary decided that there were insufficient reasons to close the fair and the local people were pleased with the outcome.

The place where Barnet fair resides has changed over the years. In 1859 the horse fair was held on land to the east of the railway, between Potters lane and the Meadway.

The Fair has had many sites including this one which is on the side where High Barnet station now is.

In 1929 development saw the fair move across Barnet hill to fields to the south of Bedford Avenue and 2 years later it moved to a field adjoining Pricklers hill.
In 1934 the fair was once again moved on due to development to field in Barnet Lane, with a the horse fair in one field and the pleasure fair in another. This is more or less where the fair as we know it today is held but the horse fair has declined over the years.

With the demise of the use of the horse it would be the pleasure fair that was to keep alive the yearly event and to this day September is the time of the year when we can walk up to our necks in mud but still enjoy a part of the past.

"Let's do a deal"

The term 'Barnet Fair', normally shortened to 'Barnet', has become rhyming slang for 'hair'.

"Barnet Fair" is the name of a song by Steeleye Span.

THE BARNET RACES

Did you know there used to be a racetrack in the town of Barnet?

By the mid-18th century Barnet fair had become associated with horse racing and races were held on the last three days of the event. The course was where the present High Barnet station now is and newspaper advertisements exist from 1751 onwards.

In 1762 William Toldervy noted *'The annual horse racing is an exhibition of bad horses, and worse riders not to be seen at any other course in England, 'Tis notorious, that more misfortunes generally happen at Barnet Races than at any other horse race whatever'.*

A decade later Horace Walpole wrote ' attended by no accident except an escape from being drowned in a torrent of whores and apprentices at Barnet races' Because the fair was popular and with large amounts of money available crime became on the increase and there was a lot of illegal gambling, the 1756 guide to Barnet races routinely recorded cockfighting results.

This did not go down well with the Barnet association.

Local associations were a standard response to law and order problems, and one was therefore formed in 1792 to cover Chipping and East Barnet. Its aim was the capture and conviction of offenders, and it was deemed so successful that in December its area was extended to cover Hadley, South Mimms and other adjacent parishes.

The Association's role, though, was limited to fund-raising and lobbying, and enforcement continued as before. They must have been relieved that the course's heyday was short lived. In 1793 The Times noted that the races had been 'miserably attended'.

In 1867 the GNR laid on special trains on the mainline, but in 1871 the new suburban line and station were being built across the track.

The last race held there was "The Barnet Stakes" on September 6th 1870 and it featured only three events, of which two were walkovers, while in the third only three horses ran, of which one bolted.

But the fair carried on and the animals kept coming, usually to the land opposite High Barnet station.
In 1888 the non-resident lord of the manor petitioned the Home Secretary to close Barnet Fair, but it was still such a vital part of the local economy that he had little support.

Some innkeepers reckoned to cover the whole of their annual rent with the fair takings pointing out that around 40,000 cattle changed hands during each fair, and that drovers and dealers, as well as other visitors, spent considerable sums locally.

"Ere older you grow, here's a song you should know,
I'd advise you to buy and to larn it,
T'other day't happened so, with a friend I did go
To see the famed races of Barnet.
Sing fol-de-rol fol-de-rol-lay."

BARNET ROAD SIGNS.

Most of know that the town of Barnet is historical and nothing says it more than the names of some of the roads around here. Below is a small section of some of them.

BOSWORTH ROAD: The Battle of Bosworth or Bosworth Field was an important battle during the Wars of the Roses in 15th century England. It was fought on 22 August 1485 between the Yorkist King Richard III, the last of the Plantagenet dynasty, and the Lancastrian contender for the crown, Henry Tudor, 2nd Earl of Richmond (later King Henry VII). It ended in the defeat and death of Richard and the establishment of the Tudor dynasty. Historically, the battle is considered to have marked the end of the Wars of the Roses.

GLOUCESTER ROAD: Richard III, the eleventh child of Richard, Duke of York, and Cecily Neville, was born in 1452. He was created third Duke of Gloucester at the coronation of his brother, Edward IV. Richard of Gloucester was crowned Richard III on July 6, 1483. He was the last of the Plantagenet dynasty, which had ruled England since 1154; and the last English king to die on the battlefield at Bosworth Field. He is credited with the responsibility for several murders including his nephews Edward and Richard (princes in the Tower).

KING EDWARD ROAD: Edward IV was born in 1442. He married Elizabeth Woodville in 1464, the widow of the Lancastrian Sir John Grey, who bore him ten children. Edward came to the throne through the efforts of his father; Richard Duke of York as his cousin Henry VI became increasingly less effective, Richard pressed the claim of the York family but was killed before he could ascend the throne: Edward deposed Henry after defeating the Lancastrians at Mortimer's Cross in 1461. Richard Neville, the Kingmaker, Earl of Warwick proclaimed Henry king once again in 1470, but less than a year elapsed when Edward reclaimed the crown and after winning the Battle of Barnet he had Henry executed in 1471.He also had his brother, George, Duke of Clarendon, murdered in 1478 on a charge of treason. His marriage to Elizabeth Woodville annoyed his councillors, and he allowed many of the great nobles to build large power bases in the provinces in return for their support.

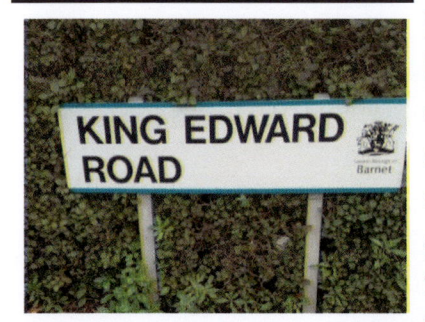

Edward died suddenly in 1483, leaving behind two son's five daughters, and a troubled kingdom.

LANCASTER ROAD: In the late 1400's the House of York fought the House of Lancaster for the English crown. Because Lancaster's heraldic badge was a red rose and York's was a white rose, the long conflict came to be known as the Wars of the Roses (1455 - 85). The wars started when the nobles of York rose against Henry VI of Lancaster who was a feeble ruler.

Edward IV, of York, replaced Henry as king. Later, Henry again became king, but lost his crown once more to Edward after the battle of Tewkesbury in 1471.This battle was the month following the Battle of Barnet where Warwick (who had changed sides to the Lancastrians) was killed .The Yorkists held power until Richard II lost his throne to the Lancastrian Henry Tudor who into the House of York. This union ended the conflict.

NORFOLK ROAD: John Mowbray, 3rd Duke of Norfolk (1415-1461) was an important player in the Wars of the Roses and he held the office of Earl Marshal from 1432, when he inherited the title of3rd Duke of Norfolk. At the beginning of the War of the Roses in 1450 he supported Richard, Duke of York, the leader of the Yorkist faction. However, in 1459, he swore allegiance to the Lancastrian Henry VI. He then quickly changed sides back to the Yorkists. This sort of treachery was by no means unusual during the Roses. In February 1461 he fought for the defeated Yorkists in the Second Battle of St Albans. In March 1461 (Richard, Duke of York now being dead) he was one of those who asked the Duke's son the Earl of March to become Edward IV and later that month his intervention at the Battle of Towton was decisive. As Earl Marshal Mowbray he then officiated at Edward IV's coronation.

NORTHUMBERLAND ROAD: John Neville. Earl of Northumberland was a Yorkist leader in the Wars of the Roses. Best-known for eliminating Lancastrian resistance during the early part of the reign of Edward IV. Montagu was a younger son of Richard Neville. 5th Earl of Salisbury and a brother of Warwick the Kingmaker He fought at the Battle of Blore Heath and was captured and imprisoned by the Lancastrians. After the Yorkist victory at Northampton he was released but was captured again at the Albans. Following his second release from imprisonment he led the Yorkist forces in the north defeating the Lancastrians at Hedgeley Moor and at Hexham (both 1465). In reward for driving out the Lancastrians. Montagu was created Earl of Northumberland. This title had long been held by the Percy family but they were in disgrace. However when Henry Percy was rehabilitated in 1470.

Montagu was forced to give up the earldom and many important offices in favour of his former enemy. He then turned against Edward IV and he joined his brother Warwick the Kingmaker in the restoration of Henry VI. He was by his brothers side when they were both killed at the Battle of Barnet.

PLANTAGENET ROAD: The Plantagenets were a dynasty of kings that ruled England for over three centuries between the years 1155 and 1485. The name Plantagenet seems to have originated as a nickname for Count Geoffrey and refers to his habit of wearing a sprig of broom flower (Latin planta genista) in his hat. Two separate branches of the family had a difference of opinion regarding which of them had a best claim to the throne and it led to Roses. This difference of opinion appeared to have been settled by the events of the years 1470 to 1471, which resulted in the deaths of the last two Lancastrian Plantagenets in Henry VI and his son Edward of Westminster. This left the three surviving sons of Richard Plantagenet, the 3rd Duke of York; being Edward, George and Richard. Edward became Edward IV who had his bother drown in a barrel of wine for treason. When Edward died Richard took over until his death at the battle of Bosworth, The legitimate male issue of the Plantagenet line became extinct with the execution in 1499 of Edward, Earl of Warwick, grandson of Richard. Duke of York.

SALISBURY ROAD: Richard Neville, Earl of Salisbury , fought on the side of the Yorkist during the War of the Roses and he was beheaded by the Lancastrians. His eldest son was the famous Earl of Warwick also known as The Kingmaker. (See Warwick Road)

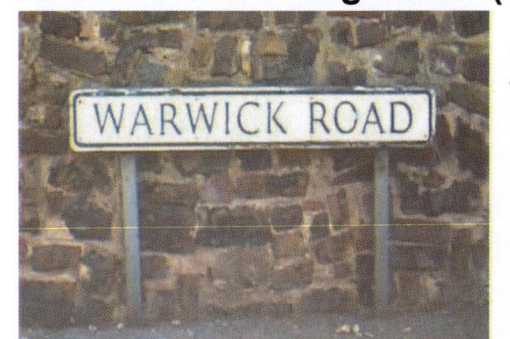

WARWICK ROAD: Commonly known as the 'Kingmaker: Richard Neville was the eldest son of his namesake. Richard Neville, 5th Earl of Salisbury the Earl of Salisbury 's sister was married to the Royal claimant. the Duke of York. He became a great supporter of the Yorkist cause and became adviser and friend to. Edward IV. He soon became the second richest and second most powerful person in the land after the king. But this friendship was to end when Edward married Elizabeth Woodville and, the favours. which he showered on her relations, soon roused the jealousy of the Earl.

This falling out led to Warwick joining the enemy forces of the Lancastrians and in April 1471 he found himself in charge of the Lancastrian army as they faced the Yorkists and his old friend at the Battle of Barnet. He is reported to have been slain somewhere near the Hadley Highstone.

WOODVILLE ROAD: Wife of Edward IV, mother of Elizabeth of York and therefore maternal grandmother of Henry VIII. Her first marriage was to Sir John Grey (by whom she had two sons) who died and left her a widow. She then married King Edward IV and bore him as many as 11 children. Even though her daughter became Henry VII's queen, she may have been involved in a treasonous plot against the king, and was deprived of her dower (1487) and retired to Bermondsey Abbey.

If you want to know more about the street names of Barnet READ "Barnet in its street names" by Doreen Wilcox, available from Barnet Museum

HADLEY CHURCH.

Hadley or Monken Hadley adjoins the town of Barnet on the north and probably owes its name to "its elevated situation, Headleagh signifying in the Saxon a high place." The manor belonged to the a family called the Mandevilles till he middle of the 12th century, when it was alienated by Geoffrey de Maneville to the Abbey of Walden hence Monken (or Monk's) Hadley.

The parish church of St Mary the Virgin (Hadley church) was built in its present form in 1494 (the date being carved in stone over the west door) although a church is believed to have stood on the site for over 800 years.

If that is the case could a church have been here during or shortly after the Battle of Barnet? Another mystery. Whatever date is it the oldest building around *Barnet?*

The present building is in the perpendicular style, and includes two side chapels (in transepts) dedicated to St Anne and St Catherine.

The building was heavily renovated in Victorian times, and contains large quantities of Victorian woodwork furniture.

The tower of the church, at the west end was probably not added until the 16th century and contains eight bells which are in good order. At the top of the tower there is a signal beacon, part of an ancient series of signal beacons

The beacon has become a symbol of the local area, and forms the badge of the nearby Church of England primary school.

There is a little grave yard next to the church and the history is all there on the tombstones. If you want to step back in time and learn more about an historical part of Barnet this church is well worth a visit.

THE GHOST OF OAKHILL PARK.

Oakhill Park is known for its football pitches, Bowling Green a children's playground and of course the East Barnet festival that is held there every year. But did you know that it also had a ghost?

The local newspaper, the Barnet Press, wrote, "Headless hounds, decapitated bodies, spectres in the trees - the list of ghostly experiences at Oak Hill Park in East Barnet seems to go on and on."

One of them comes in the shape of a medieval knight riding on a horse and the story is that it is Sir Geoffrey de Mandeville whose grandfather fought at the Battle of Hastings. For his gallantry William the Conquer rewarded him with large areas of land in Essex and Middlesex, Many years later and his grandson, also named Sir Geoffrey de Mandeville, was awarded the title of Earl of Essex by King Stephen.

By 1141 Sir Geoffrey had become the most powerful baron in England but it was not long before he fell out with Stephen. Once his friend he was now his enemy and he became an outlaw.

In 1144 Sir Geoffrey was slain by an arrow in a skirmish against the king but because he had been excommunicated he was denied a Christianity burial so his body was wrapped in lead and taken to the Templar community in London.

He was buried in the Temple Church in London (which was featured in the Da Vinci Code) and you can still see an effigy of him on the floor of that building.

Why he decided to haunt East Barnet (it is also reported that he haunts Hadley woods) is a mystery and why people have thought he was Sir Geoffrey is also strange.

Perhaps a different view would be that he was one of the knights at the Battle of Barnet which would be a better reason for why he is a knight and also have link to Barnet history.

Whoever he is he is not the only ghost that apparently visits our local park.

Church Hill Road, which runs alongside Oak Hill Park, was known as "The Ghosts' Promenade", because of the many supernatural sightings. Although I can find no other named ghosts (other than Sir Geoffrey) reported as haunting the park there must have been more sighting over the years for it to get such a reputation.

There was in fact another strange incident that happened in Oakhill.

In the early 1930s an old oak tree in the Park burst into flames on a clear summer day. No one knew what caused it but this particular tree had a story as it was the actual oak tree under which the famous 18th century religious prophetess Joanna Southcott (1750 – 1814) used to sit during her many visits to friends in East Barnet and it was here that she had many visions.

She was such an eccentric that at the age of 64 she announced she was going to give birth to a Messiah but she died shortly after that without fulfilling her prophecy.

So be careful if you take a short cut through the park, especially if you have had a few too many at the Prince as you just might come across a man on a horse whose spirit lives on.

To know more about this and more local history go to the ultimate Barnet history site @ www.barnet4u.co.uk.

GENERAL MONCK'S VISIT TO BARNET.

As with the battle of 1471, so General Monck's eventful night in Barnet in 1660 was entirely due to the road. On 2 February, in the final phase before the restoration of Charles 11, Monck marched southwards from St Albans and stayed overnight at Barnet, probably at the Mitre. One of his chaplains, John Price, recorded that the general *'took up quarters only for himself and his entourage...much business was here dispacht; orders were distributed for our next day's march into town (London) and that our soldiers should demean themselves civily in their quarters, and pay for them; for our money held out still'*.

The alternative scenario if military money had run out hovers like a chill in the air, not least because Price reported that *'The next day, before we came to Highgate, the general drew up his forces, which consisted of four regiments of foot and three of horse their number being 5,800, allowing 1,000 to each regiment of foot and 600 to each regiment of horse, besides officers'*.

This time, though, the excitement was limited to Thomas Scot, one of the commissioners sent by Parliament to keep Monck under surveillance, who at around midnight burst in after what must have been a brisk run through the streets, clad only in night gown, cap and slippers, to relay news from London that soldiers there 'were fallen into a high mutiny, and that there was a danger that they would joyn with the apprentices, who cryed upon the streets for a Free Parliament, and passionately desired, or rather by his authority required the general immediately to *beat his drums and march'*.

Keeping his head, Monck 'calmly answered him, *I will answer for this night's disturbance and be early enough in the morning to prevent any mischief'*. He did agree to send a messenger immediately, who reported that the uproar had been soon quashed, thus strengthening the suspicion that Scot's dramatic performance *and' motion for such a hasty march was... an artifice. .so as to mingle the soldiers of both armies that they might be the less at the general's devotion'*.

How all Monck's troops were billeted is hard to imagine, but a century later the War Office billeting returns of 1756 offer a handy guide to the Barnet and Hadley inns.

Monck entered London on February 3rd, 1660

Monck signing the declaration which paved the way for the restoration of the monarchy in the person of Charles II.

THE OLD PHYSIC WELL.

Man: *Hello Mr. Pepys, Have you come to take the water again?*
Pepys: *Yes my man and it's worth a note in my diary*!

That probably never happened but Samuel Pepys did visit the well on Well house lane back in the 17th century. What was the well? Well, it served a spring and its water was supposed to have therapeutic qualities.
In 1586 a William Camden wrote: "*Upon the south border (of Hertfordshire) was discovered a medicinal spring which is of great service to the sex where there is general languor, difficult respiration, febile heat and loss of appetite. In all colds and fevers and rheumatic complaints. The Barnet whey is much recommended.*"
Perhaps it did not catch on as, over 60 years later in 1652, it was reported in a journal:
"*There is lately found at Barnet, 10 miles from London an excellent purging water. It springs from a nitre mine and half the quantity works as effectively as that of Epsom. It is much approved of by several eminent physicians and those that have occasion to use it may repair there for free.*"

From around that time the well became popular and in 1661 the Reverend Joshua Childrey declared in his book "*Natural Rarities of England, Scotland and Wales*" that The Barnet mineral waters: "*Were very famous.* You could buy spirits and tobacco from a house beside the well and it seems like someone had a nice little sideline to cater for the ladies and gentlemen who traveled from London on a daily basis.

People were allowed to take water from the well, except in casks which could have been due to this 1663 advert for The Angel and Sun, an inn on the Thames: "*Constantly to be sold, all the year, fresh Tunbridge Water and Epsom Water and Barnet water and Epsom ale and Spruce beer*

In July 1664 Samuel Pepys made his first visit to the well and he drank five glasses and wrote: *"The woman (the attendant) would have me drink three more, but I could not."*

On 11th August 1667 he visited the well at about seven o'clock in the morning and said: *"Many people were a drinking"*
From there he went into Barnet where he took tea and cakes.

Samuel Pepys

The popularity of the well lasted until the end of the 18th century with sometimes up to thirty carriages on hand to take people to and from the well.

Off to take the water at Barnet

In 1808 a Mr. Sorrell, a Barnet chemist was selling the water over the counter and probably chemists elsewhere were doing the same. Perhaps it was easier to buy bottle of water rather than go to the well and by 1840 it was reported that "the well house" had been demolished, and the well covered over and that only a small pump was visible.

The physic well to the right, from a watercolour of c.1790.

The farmer of the well house field where it was situated painted the pump green to deter people walking across his land. In time the well was forgotten except by a few locals.

In 1907 the Hertfordshire county analyst declared that the water was: *"Unfit for drinking and did not posses any medicinal properties."*

In 1922 another analysts report said that: "The water retained its high medicinal properties, was remarkably uncontaminated and safe to drink."

Either way, it was not to matter as, in the 1930s, the Well house estate was built around the well and in 1937 the present building was erected to cover it. Although threatened with demolition over the years, it still remains to remind us of a time when Barnet was the fashionable place to take "The Waters"

The Well today

DAVID LIVINGSTONE.

David Livingstone was born on March 19, 1813, in Blantyre, Scotland. His parents were devout Christians and they played an important role in his life by introducing him to the subject of missions. By the time he turned twenty one, Livingstone had accepted Christ and made up his mind to become a medical missionary. He studied Latin, medicine, theology and Squirrel Anatomy (!) at the University of Glasgow and applied to join the London Missionary Society where he was accepted for missionary training. After completing his medical course in 1840, Livingstone was ordained and sent as a medical missionary to South Africa. In 1841 he reached Kuruman, a settlement in Bechuanaland (now Botswana).

This is where he met his wife Mary in 1845 and they had six children. Livingstone often took his family with him while crossing the African wilderness but there were many times when they could not be together. The longest period of separation was for five years between November of 1853 and May 1856 when Livingstone completed one of the most amazing journeys ever undertaken, a coast to coast venture that covered four thousand miles of unexplored land, most of which was located along the Zambezi River. He was the first European to see the Mosi-oa-Tunya ("the smoke that thunders") waterfall (which he renamed Victoria Falls after his monarch, Queen Victoria).

Livingstone's house In Hadley

After sixteen years Livingstone made his first visit to England in 1856 and from 1857-8, he lived in the house at Hadley where he finished his first book, "Missionary Travels,"
Livingstone was a national hero and he was honoured by the Royal Geographical Society and was received by the men of science, the Queen and the royal family.

~ 70 ~

He was also was given the freedom of the cities of London, Edinburgh, and Glasgow and honours of the Universities of Glasgow, and Oxford, and Cambridge.

But Livingstone missed Africa and on March 10, 1858, with his wife and their son Oswell, they sailed from England.

At Cape Town Mrs. Livingstone became so ill that she had to remain behind while he was establishing sites for missions, preaching the Gospel, healing the sick, and contributing religious and scientific articles to periodicals in England.

In 1862 Mary died and Livingstone continued his expeditions, returning to England for the last time in 1864No European had ever explored North Africa and this would his next venture when he returned to Africa in 1866. Marching inland he reached Lake Nyasson and began journeying north toward Lake Tanganyika. Months rolled by and then years without the outside world knowing where he was. This is when a New York reporter, Henry Morton Stanley, accepted the challenge to "Find Livingstone." On November 10, 1871, Stanley's caravan, loaded with supplies, reached Ujiji, Africa.

A thin, frail Livingstone stepped out to meet him as Stanley bowed, took off his hat, and spoke the now famous words, "Dr. Livingstone, I presume."

David Livingstone died on April 30, 1873, after a long illness. His heart remained in Africa but his body along with his belongings, papers and maps was transported to England, where he is buried in Westminster Abbey. His motto, inscribed in the base of the statue to him at Victoria Falls, was "Christianity, Commerce and Civilization"

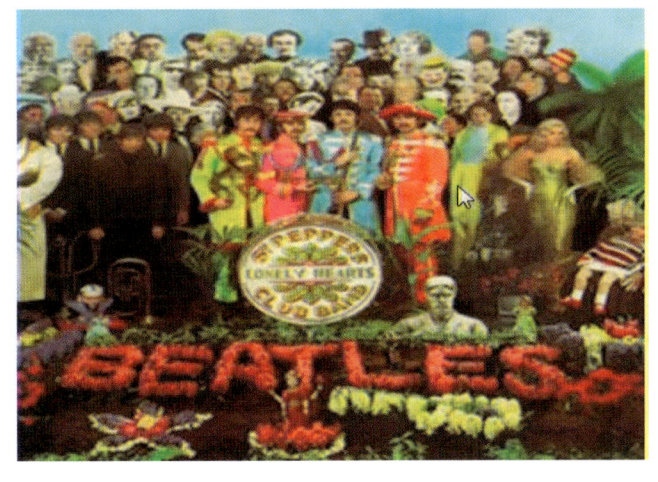

OLIVER TWIST MEETS THE ARTFUL DODGER IN BARNET HIGH STREET.

Oliver Twist by Charles Dickens is one of the most famous books in the world and it has been filmed many times and is also a hit musical. But what would have happened to Oliver if he had not gone through Barnet or if the Artful Dodger was not in the town at that time. He would not have meet Fagan and his adventures may not have happened. So Barnet has its place in English Literature as well as its place in English history.

Chapter VIII   OLIVER WALKS TO LONDON. HE ENCOUNTERS ON THE ROAD A STRANGE SORT OF YOUNG GENTLEMAN

Early on the seventh morning after he had left his native place, Oliver limped slowly into the little town of Barnet. The window-shutters were closed; the street was empty; not a soul had awakened to the business of the day. The sun was rising in all its splendid beauty; but the light only served to show the boy his own lonesomeness and desolation, as he sat, with bleeding feet and covered with dust, upon a door-step. By degrees, the shutters were opened; the window-blinds were drawn up; and people began passing to and fro. Some few stopped to gaze at Oliver for a moment or two, or turned round to stare at him as they hurried by; but none relieved him, or troubled themselves to inquire how he came there. He had no heart to beg. And there he sat. He had been crouching on the step for some time: wondering at the great number of public-houses (every other house in Barnet was a tavern, large or small), gazing listlessly at the coaches as they passed through, and thinking how strange it seemed that they could do, with ease, in a few hours, what it had taken him a whole week of courage and determination beyond his years to accomplish: when he was roused by observing that a boy, who had passed him carelessly some minutes before, had returned, and was now surveying him most earnestly from the opposite side of the way. He took little heed of this at first; but the boy remained in the same attitude of close observation so long, that Oliver raised his head, and returned his steady look.

Upon this, the boy crossed over; and walking close up to Oliver, said 'Hullo, my covey! What's the row?'
The boy, who addressed this inquiry to the young wayfarer, was about his own age: but one of the queerest looking boys that Oliver had even seen. He was a snub-nosed, flat-browed, common-faced boy enough; and as dirty a juvenile as one would wish to see; but he had about him all the airs and manners of a man. He was short of his age: with rather bow-legs, and little, sharp, ugly eyes. His hat was stuck on the top of his head so lightly, that it threatened to fall off every moment--and would have done so, very often, if the wearer had not had a knack of every now and then giving his head a sudden twitch, which brought it back to its old place again.

He wore a man's coat, which reached nearly to his heels. He had turned the cuffs back, half-way up his arm, to get his hands out of the sleeves: apparently with the ultimated view of thrusting them into the pockets of his corduroy trousers; for there he kept them.
He was, altogether, as roystering and swaggering a young gentleman as ever stood four feet six, or something less, in the bluchers. 'Hullo, my covey! What's the row?' said this strange young gentleman to Oliver. 'I am very hungry and tired,' replied Oliver: the tears standing in his eyes as he spoke. 'I have walked a long way. I have been walking these seven days.'
'Walking for sivin days!' said the young gentleman. 'Oh, I see. Beak's order, eh? But,' he added, noticing Oliver's look of surprise, 'I suppose you don't know what a beak is, my flash com-pan-i-on.' Oliver mildly replied that he had always heard a bird's mouth described by the term in question.
'My eyes, how green!' exclaimed the young gentleman. 'Why, a beak's a madgst'rate; and when you walk by a beak's order, it's not straight forerd, but always agoing up, and niver a coming down agin. Was you never on the mill?'
'What mill?' inquired Oliver.
'What mill! Why, THE mill--the mill as takes up so little room that it'll work inside a Stone Jug; and always goes better when the wind's low with people, than when it's high; acos then they can't get workmen. But come,' said the young gentleman; 'you want grub, and you shall have it. I'm at low-water-mark myself--only one bob and a magpie; but,

as far as it goes, I'll fork out and stump. Up with you on your pins. There! Now then! Morrice!'

Assisting Oliver to rise, the young gentleman took him to an adjacent chandler's shop, where he purchased a sufficiency of ready-dressed ham and a half-quarter loaf, or, as he himself expressed it, 'a fourpenny bran!' the ham being kept clean and preserved from dust, by the ingenious expedient of making a hole in the loaf by pulling out a portion of the crumb, and stuffing it therein.

Taking the bread under his arm, the young gentleman turned into a small public-house, and led the way to a tap-room in the rear of the premises. Here, a pot of beer was brought in, by direction of the mysterious youth; and Oliver, falling to, at his new friend's bidding, made a long and hearty meal, during the progress of which the strange boy eyed him from time to time with great attention.

'Going to London?' said the strange boy, when Oliver had at length concluded. 'Yes.'

'Got any lodgings?'

'No.'

'Money?'

'No.'

The strange boy whistled; and put his arms into his pockets, as far as the big coat-sleeves would let them go.

'Do you live in London?' inquired Oliver.

'Yes. I do, when I'm at home,' replied the boy. 'I suppose you want some place to sleep in to-night, don't you?'

'I do, indeed,' answered Oliver. 'I have not slept under a roof since I left the country.'

'Don't fret your eyelids on that score.' said the young gentleman. 'I've got to be in London to-night; and I know a 'spectable old gentleman as lives there, wot'll give you lodgings for nothink, and never ask for the change, that is, if any genelman he knows interduces you. And don't he know me? Oh, no!

Not in the least! By no means. Certainly not!'

The young gentleman smiled, as if to intimate that the latter fragments of discourse were playfully ironical; and finished the beer as he did so. This unexpected offer of shelter was too tempting to be resisted; especially as it was immediately followed up, by the assurance that the *old gentleman referred to, would doubtless provide Oliver with a comfortable place, without loss of time.*

This led to a more friendly and confidential dialogue; from which Oliver discovered that his friend's name was Jack Dawkins, and that he was a peculiar pet and protege of the elderly gentleman before mentioned.

Mr. Dawkin's appearance did not say a vast deal in favour of the comforts which his patron's interest obtained for those whom he took under his protection; but, as he had a rather flightly and dissolute mode of conversing, and furthermore avowed that among his intimate friends he was better known by the sobriquet of 'The Artful Dodger,'

Oliver concluded that, being of a dissipated and careless turn, the moral precepts of his benefactor had hitherto been thrown away upon him. Under this impression, he secretly resolved to cultivate the good opinion of the old gentleman as quickly as possible; and, if he found the Dodger incorrigible, as he more than half suspected he should, to decline the honour of his farther acquaintance.

As John Dawkins objected to their entering London before nightfall, it was nearly eleven o'clock when they reached the turnpike at Islington.

*

Barnet is also mentioned in "War of the Worlds" by H.G. Wells
* Bleak House by Charles Dickens   * Tom Jones by Henry Fielding

THE LOCAL CINEMAS.

Before the advent of every home having a television the most popular form of entertainment was a trip to the cinema and there was a lot of choice.

There was the Gaumont (now the Arts Centre) and the Odeon (was a furniture shop.) in Finchley, the Bohemia in Church End and the Rex (now the Phoenix) in East Finchley.

FINCHLEY ODEON **FINCHLEY GAUMONT** **EAST FINCHLEY REX**

Barnet's own earliest was the Cinema Palace, opened in the silent era on 26th December 1912 with all seating on a single floor. It was renamed the Barnet Cinema in 1926, when it was operating two evening houses and a Saturday matinee. Taken over by the Odeon circuit in 1936 and renamed the Gaumont in 1955, it closed in 1959. It was demolished in 1961 and a Waitrose supermarket was built on the site, later an Iceland store.

BARNET GAUMONT

Located in the East Barnet. The Dominion Cinema was opened on 31st October 1938 with film star Gracie Fields appearing in person before a huge crowd. Taken over by the Newcastle upon Tyne based chain, it was re-named the Essoldo on 22nd January 1950. It became the first of London's suburban cinemas to screen Cinemascope when "Flight of the White Heron" was screened in June 1954. The Essoldo was closed on 21st January 1967 with Audrey Hepburn in "My Fair Lady". The final performance was a total 'sell out'. The cinema was demolished and a supermarket was built on the site.

In New Barnet the Lytton Road Assembly Rooms (built by E. Fergusson Taylor c.1870) were converted into a small cinema, the Hippodrome, which ran for three months in 1925, was re launched later the same year as the Kinema, and was then replaced with a purpose-built house, the New Barnet Picture Theatre, in 1926.

It became the Regal in 1933 and was converted to bingo in 1966 and quasar thereafter, before demolition in 1999.

Barnet Odeon **Opening Day**

The Odeon Theatre, Barnet opened on 15th May 1935 with Gene Raymond in "Transatlantic Merry-Go-Round" and Laurel & Hardy in "Them Thar' Hills". It was designed by architect Edgar J. Simmons, who was not a usual designer of Odeon Theatres, as this was originally intended to be a building for County Cinemas circuit and was taken over by Odeon during construction. Seating was provided for 1,553; 1,010 in the stalls and 543 in the circle.

It was converted into a triple screen cinema from 10th March 1974 with screen 1 in the former circle and screens 2 and 3 in the rear stalls. On 18th December 1989, the Odeon Barnet was given a Grade II Listed building status by English Heritage.

From 18th December 1992 a fourth screen was added in the former front stalls area and ten days later a fifth screen was opened on what had been the former stage area.

It continues to serve this local outer North London suburb of Barnet as a first run cinema. In April 2015 it was announced that the Everyman Cinemas chain was purchasing the Odeon. It was re-named Everyman in July 2015 and was refurbished in early-May 2016.

FILM MAKERS IN BARNET
BIRT ACRES (1854 – 1918)

Birt Acres was the first man to successfully take and project a 35 mm film in England. And he lived in Barnet.

He was born to English parents in America and when or why he arrived in England is not clear but it is known he took up the profession of photographer in London. In 1892, he became manager of Elliott and Sons Ltd, manufacturers of the famous Barnet Dry Plates and he and his wife lived in Clovelly Cottage, the manager's house next to the factory in Park Road.

In December 1894, he was approached by the engineer and instrument-maker Robert Paul, who had begun to produce replicas of Edison Kinetoscopes and needed someone with photographic expertise to collaborate on the production of a camera.

Together they developed a ciné camera and by February 1895 made their first film experiment, showing their mutual friend Henry Short walking outside Clovelly Cottage, Acres' home in Barnet, wearing cricket whites. This untitled test film, never exhibited commercially, was the first true British film production. And it happened in Barnet.

Using his portable cinematograph camera Acres began to build a portfolio of 35mm films which included 'The Henley Royal Regatta of 1895 and the University Boat Race of 1895.

Early in 1895 Acres left Elliott's and established his own company, The Northern Photographic Works, first at 45 Salisbury Road, later as a limited company at Nesbitts Alley, Barnet, where he developed his improved film projector Kineopticon. When the film industry became a booming business, Birt Acres expanded his activities and the Northern Photographic Works became the Whetstone

Birt Acres and his wife

Photographic Works Ltd, moving at the same time to much bigger premises at Whetstone.

In August 1895, he gave his first semi-public film show at the Assembly Rooms in New Barnet, but it was not until the beginning of 1896 that Birt Acres felt confident enough to give a public exhibition of his 'animated photography', as it was then called.

He showed his films to the Lyonsdown Amateur Photographic Association in Barnet on the 10th of January. This was certainly the first successful screen projection of films in England.

And it happened in Barnet.

Filmed outside his cottage in Park Road

Acres and Paul split acrimoniously that July, and continued to attack each other through the photographic press as each made their separate way toward projected film and the emergence of a British cinema business.

Acres swiftly slid from the scene, and ceased film production soon after 1900. He continued in film processing and celluloid manufacture, but was unlucky in business and was twice made bankrupt. He died in Whitechapel, London on 27 December 1918.

Clovelly Cottage today
(And why is there not a blue plaque there?)

FILM MAKERS IN BARNET
LOTTE REINIGER (1899-1981)

Through double iron gates, up a long gravel drive and somewhere here among the very tall trees of 89 Park Road, Barnet was once the film studio of Lotte Reiniger.

Lotte with her husband Carl Koch pioneered the development of the animated film in Berlin before coming to England in 1934.

Known all over the world for her silhouette and coloured flat-figure films, this distinguished artist/animator for many years, worked from her studio in New Barnet.

It was in 1923-26 that Lotte Reiniger with her husband made the first ever full feature length silhouette film 'The Adventures of Prince Achmed', a milestone in film history; while Disney was still experimenting with short films. "

The coloured figures for Lotte's films were usually cut from transparent coloured plastic sheets known as cinemoid, while the opaque black figures were sometimes made from thin lead or cardboard; all with movable joints. The backgrounds being made from paper of varying thickness and translucence and the scenes were photographed frame by frame from above a 'table' lit from below. This process required incredible patience and dexterity.

A memory from Reg Lodge Art Director on "Yellow Submarine"

On 13th July, 1974 a 75th Birthday tribute was held at the Odeon cinema Barnet. I was invited along by film critic Paul Gelder who had taken an interest in my work as Animator/Director and he introduced me to Lotte; who I found to be a most friendly and charming lady. I recall Lotte saying she had seen and enjoyed the 'Beatles' film 'Yellow Submarine' and she wanted to hear how we had produced the Polarized light effects used in this production. I also recall her mentioning that many negatives of her early films were destroyed during the 1945 battle for Berlin.

I understand that there does exist somewhere, a short documentary film 'The Art of Lotte Reiniger', all about her work made in 1970 produced and directed by Louis Hagen.

WHERE DID THE BOMBS DROP IN BARNET?

By Roger Aitken

East Barnet Urban District Council Bomb Plan (1939-45) *Displayed on the first floor at the Barnet Museum, just off the High Street, are two district council maps pinpointing where German bombs landed around High Barnet and East Barnet during World War Two (1939-45). According to Mr McCall, a museum volunteer and member of the Barnet History Society, a parachute landmine got caught in a tree near Hampden Square where he lived in early days of 1941. At the time Mr McCall was in the navy. Visitors can see views the maps and through the aid of a magnifying glass can revel in the myriad of bombs that landed across the EN4 area. A range of different coloured pins identify where incendiaries landed and the findings might make some of the younger generation realise just how lucky they are to be alive today. In total 200 houses were damaged and "beyond repair" in the East Barnet district between 1939-45, with 405 described as "seriously" damaged and 13,878 just slightly.

These guns were used to defend Barnet

Around the edges of Oak Hill Park, near East Barnet Village, a whole plethora of German bombs were despatched. For example, one red pin indicates 'Kilo1' incendiary bomb dropped and located in the park near what is a nature trail through a middle age forest adjacent to the defunct bandstand. A notation indicates that the group of Kilo1. Bombs were "too numerous to plot", with approximately 3,700 said to have been dropped in the area by the Nazis.

Elsewhere in the park, a light blue pin reveals that an anti-aircraft missile landed (a total of 40 such missiles were found across the district. High explosive bombs, which are marked by dark blue pins, were fairly prevalent during the period too, with 98 in total falling in the district and three in East Barnet village. In total 3,859 bombs were said to have been discovered (or fallen) in the district in the six year period, killing 53 people, seriously wounding 348 and slightly wounding 454 - making a total of 855 casualties to one degree or another. A flying bomb (aka FBs) or Doodlebugs - seven in number for the district - can be on the edge of the park. And, several other types of bombs littered streets near St Mary's Church, which dates back to 1090.

~ 83 ~

A pin on the map also signifies that near the grounds of the theological college in Chase Side, a bomb was located.

Looking at specifically roads in East Barnet, one discovers on closer inspection that a bomb landed in what appears to be the back garden of a house in the middle of Jackson Road; another on the corner where Capel Road meets Rosslyn Road.

A long-range rocket was found in a residential area a stones throw from Longmore Avenue on the side above the Post Office after the railway bridge. Oil bombs and PMs, parachute mines, were common across the district. The London & North East Railway line, which is the route from London to the North of England, was extremely fortunate not to see the track destruction. In at least two places around where the line cuts through New Barnet, bombs landed within a whisker of the track itself. Also on display at the museum is the leather glove of a German Zeppelin pilot, which was discovered in a field in Cuffley after the Zeppelin, was shot down on 3, September 1916.

World War Two damage in Bells Hill

Roger Aitken is a freelance journalist who lives in East Barnet.

WHY BOMB BARNET?

We might wonder why anyone would want to bomb a quiet suburb like Barnet but during the Second World War the German air force managed to do damage in our little town at the end of the Northern line. In the first weeks of the bombing raids in September 1940 over 13.999 tons of bombs fell on London with many civilians killed, London was a main target because of the docks and the close proximity of many important building but out here in the town the people felt safe in the knowledge that there was no need for the Luftwaffe to visit Barnet as there was nothing worthwhile bombing. Or was there?

As far back as 1939 the Barnet Urban District Council were preparing for war with 218 people in training to be air raid wardens. How our council knew the war was coming is another matter but the point is we were ready! We do not know where the first bomb fell in the town but a parachute mine landed on Oakmere, an old peoples home in Bells Hill Street on November 940, killing 17 people and injuring 31 others, including nurses.

This is the devastation caused by the land mine that hit Oakmere

We also know that a bomb was dropped on some bungalows in Barnet High Road in January 1941, which killed seven people including a baby and on 20th January 1945 a V 2 rocket caused large damage and loss of life in Carlton Road East Barnet.

As you can see by the adjoining article quite a few bombs fell in the district and when the V 1 and V2 (flying bombs) started flying over this country everybody was a risk when the engine stopped and fell to whatever was below.

The distinction between tactical and strategic bombing is that strategic bombing missions usually attack targets such as factories, railroads, oil refineries and cities, while tactical bombing missions attack targets such as troop concentrations, airfields, and ammunition dumps. So it can be safely said that we did not fall under any of those categories although the Standard Telephone Company down at Brunswick Park could have been a strategic bombing. In that case there would be bombers and flying bombs in the area, in which case it is likely that quite a few of the bomber crews just dropped their cargo as near as possible and got out of there as quick as possible for the long journey back to Germany.

If you want to know more about this subject you can buy "BARNET AT WAR" by Percy Reboul and John Heathfield from The Barnet Museum.

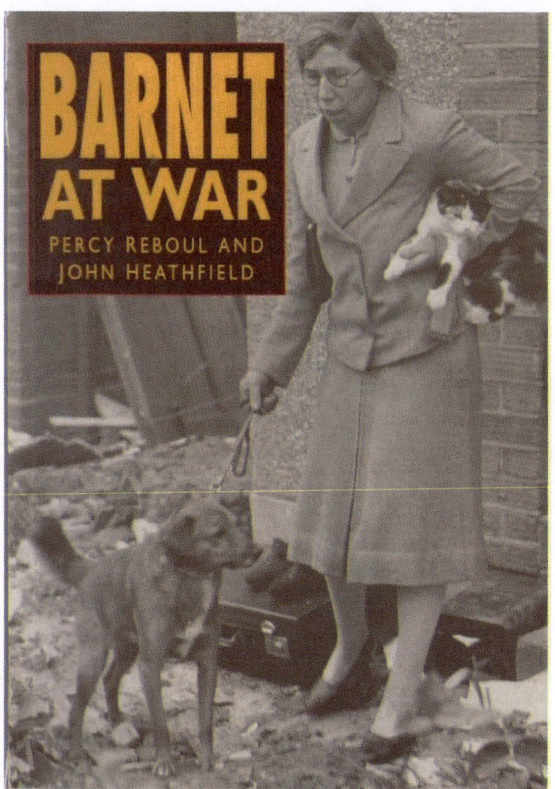

ARKLEY VIEW AND THE RADIO SECURITY SERVICE.

During World War II the Government decided to use amateur radio hams to monitor the enemy. This is their story and how Arkley played an important part in that war.

The Radio Society of Great Britain was approached with a request to sound out trusted radio amateurs to see if listening could be arranged on a voluntary basis. In time a few hundred amateurs were asked to listen on HF for anything they could not recognise as genuine commercial or military transmissions and send them in by post written on a log sheet provided, that showed date, time, frequency and what was heard.

A few experienced people in Wormwood Scrubs checked the resulting logs and notified the amateur where they were not wanted or further intercepts were required. The organization was given the title of the Radio Security Service (RSS). When the RSS was taken over by M.I.6 or Secret Intelligence Service (SIS) as it was widely known it moved on October 3rd 1940 into new headquarters at Arkley View, within a large site 2 miles north of Barnet.

This building was already being used by the Post Office as an intercept station. The 'View' housed the analysis, intelligence, direction finding control and various administrative departments. Huts were erected in the grounds for intercept work, a tele-printing terminal, and later the ever-expanding departments to identify, classify and collate the enormous secret intelligence enemy radio networks.

The secret cryptic address became well known to the select as PO Box 25 Barnet.

Arkley View was on the right of Barnet Road leading to Stirling Corner. Arkley Lane had the View on its left and Oaklands to its right. Here was accommodated the orderly room and the dispatch riders' base for taking intercepted messages to Bletchley Park. Officers' and sergeants' messes were in Scotswood opposite the View.

Other large houses such as Rowley Lodge, The Lawns and Meadowbank were used as billets, messing, transmitting and training schools. In Ravenscroft Park, High Barnet, a billet, operators' evaluation and a small intercept training station were established. Reports from interceptors came to Arkley where, after processing as explained below, copies of the same messages from different intercepts were compared to enable a good copy to be forwarded to Bletchley Park. Initially the intercepted messages came in from the VIS, working at home in complete secrecy and using whatever time was available. Many had full-time employment but others who were retired or disabled could devote more time to listening on the receivers that they had previously used as Radio Amateurs.

At Arkley it was realised that for full coverage of the ever expanding German secret networks some form of 24 hour watch was required and in different parts of the UK in order to maximise the amount of information we could obtain. It was important to find out who was 'working' to whom. As the frequencies and call signs were constantly changing the only common factor was time and possibly operating procedure. Types of preamble and times and frequencies had to be memorised by the staff, who used card indexes for reference. This work could be tedious and tiring as hundreds of log sheets were scrutinised for the brief suspect transmission.

When war finally did break out, all amateur transmitting, equipment was confiscated by the Government, but leaving selected radio amateurs (the VIs) with receivers so that they could still listen in. During his period of being a VI, When the Germans were dropping incendiary bombs on London, it was decided to move the R.S.S. out of central London to Arkley, Barnet, North London, where six big houses had been requisitioned by the government and a number of Nissan huts set up to house the radio equipment that was to be used to intercept enemy messages in morse.
The morse messages that were intercepted at Arkley were taken down in code in five letter groups and sent to Bletchley Park, (which later became GCHQ) and where the messages were decoded by the young mathematical brains of the country (Alan Turing being one), and where

the German enigma machine code was cracked using the world's first computer, Colossus.

There is no doubt that without the dedicated work of the RSS, the war would have dragged on for another two or three years as it was the work of the RSS at Arkley to concentrate on the German radio spy network (the Abwehr) which was It is sadly only in the last decade that former workers at Bletchley Park, Arkley and Hanslope Park have been able to get to know each other because of the oath of secrecy that all of them took, and because after the second world war and before the cold war with Russia, Churchill had Arkley, (the headquarters of the R.S.S. and where the most secret work was carried out), raised to the ground and all records, drawings diagrams etc. destroyed as a precautionary measure, together with the world's first programmable computer, Colossus, which was at Bletchley Park. A replica of this is currently being re-created at Bletchley Park without the aid of the original diagrams that were also destroyed.

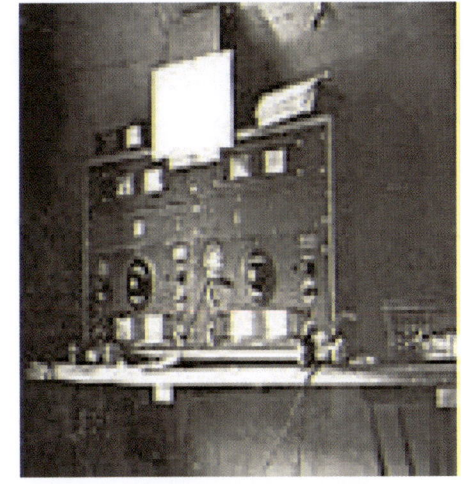

DID WINSTON CHURCHILL MEET RUDOLPH HESS IN WHETSTONE?

Winston Churchill

Rudolf Hess

When a local paper unearthed a letter in Barnet Council's planning archives that read "We purchased 'Tower House' in 1953 and have operated from here ever since. It was built many years ago as a private house.

In 1939 it was a boys' boarding school. During the war it was at different times a blood transfusion centre, a fire service station (hence the corrugated iron sheds) and a prisoner of war cage (Hess was brought here for interrogation after he flew to Scotland). After that it was unoccupied and derelict until we took it over."

It opened up a mystery. Was the letter genuine?

It was written in 1987 by Mr W Jones, the owner of Tower House, 17 Oakleigh Park North. In it he informed his neighbours that he wanted to demolish the building and erect luxury apartments in its place.

As he was the managing director of WH Jones and Co, an export, finance and banking company run from the four-store building, and that he later went on to stand as a Liberal Democrat for the Chipping Barnet seat does not mean that all this is not a lie or a prank and perhaps if anyone knows him we could add to this history.

Historians are sceptical, and say that Churchill and Hess never met, but if they had it would have been in secret and not of general knowledge. Rudolph Hess was Adolf Hitler's Deputy and no one really knows why he decided to fly solo to Scotland in 1941, where he was captured and imprisoned in The Tower of London.

It would have been unthinkable if the public thought that Churchill was meeting Hess to do a deal as at that time England was on her knees and left alone to fight Nazism so perhaps Hess came with an offer. It is hard to believe that a prime minister of a country would not be curious and want to meet the enemy face to face.

On Guard at Trent Park

During the war construction workers built living quarters, kitchens, showers and toilets which could have been used by the fire station or as a safe house. The question there is why they did not interrogate prisoners of war in one of the big houses in Totteridge or Hampstead.

Perhaps a reason why this building could have been used is that it is quite near Trent Park.

In the early twentieth century, this was owned by Philip Sassoon (the cousin of the poet Siegfried Sassoon), and he entertained many famous names at Trent park including Winston Churchill.

During World War II. Trent Park was used as a prisoner of war camp for captured German Generals and Staff Officers. They were treated well with special rations of whisky and regular walks on the grounds of The Park.

Captured German officers photographed at Trent Park

Un-be known to the Germans the camp was wired with hidden microphones and listening devices so that the British military was able to gather important military information. This is only up the road from where the most important prisoner of war was supposed to have been interrogated. Would it not have been ideal and near those interrogators that were up at Trent Park?

Whatever the truth strange other things were happening in Oakleigh Park North during the Second World War.

Trent Park World War II prisoner of war camp

BARNET PARKS AND OPEN SPACES.

Our Town of Barnet is lucky enough to not only to be surrounded by country side but also to have an abundance of lovely parks that are within walking distance for most of the population.

Up by the Hadley pond you can take a walk through KING GEORGE'S FIELDS (Boswell Road / Hadley Common) where you get a panoramic view of the capital while standing on part of the Battle of Barnet battlefield.

It is one of many King George's Fields all over the country, established as memorials, following the death of King George V in 1936. King George's Fields (has been legally protected since July 1955.

Take a walk along Wood Street and you can relax in RAVENSCROFT PARK or walk through the picturesque OLD COURT HOUSE PARK.
Originally a pasture with stables and a brewery, Barnet Urban District Council purchased the buildings in 1912 and the county court was held there till the start of WW1. The remainder of the estate was bought in 1923 and opened to the public the following year. 
The park was formally laid out with an ornamental pond, rockery, shrub and flower beds, and a fine variety of specimen trees.

HIGHLANDS GARDEN (Leicester Road/Abbotts Road) that was well known years ago for its palm trees and waterfall. Local residents are restoring it to its former beauty.
* see page 95 for more details.

Opposite The Hole in the Wall Café on the great north road is GREENHILL PARK with its lake full of wildlife and its tranquillity.

It was created from part of the former Greenhill estate, the rest of which was developed for housing in the twentieth century. In July 1926 East Barnet Council purchased the land which is now a public park for £20,000. In 1965 East Barnet became part of the London Borough of Barnet, which now owns and manages the park. There is access from Pricklers Hill and Greenhill Park.

If it's a park with more amenities that you are looking for there is the choice of TUDOR PARK (Clifford Road) with its golf and children's playground or

The park has a cricket pitch, drop-in tennis court and a basketball shooting area. There are two children's play areas - one for smaller children and a separate area for older children. The space is also is home to a 18 hole footgolf course, a café and a changing room/pavilion dating from 1920.

VICTORIA PARK (Victoria Road/ Park Road/Lawton Road) which also has a playground plus tennis and bowls. There are football pitches here.

The park was laid out in the late nineteenth century on land previously known as 'Mrs Cook's Farm', and Barnet Football Club played there in the 1889–90 season. The Shirebourne brook runs along the south side of the park and the Pymmes Brook Trail passes north–south through the park.

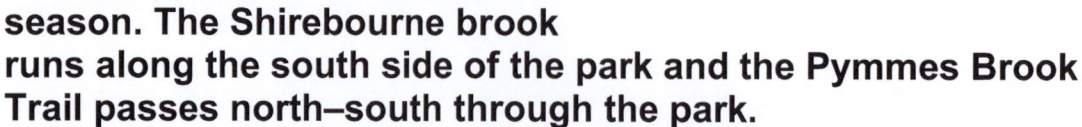

There is access from Park Road, Victoria Road, Lawton Road, and by a footpath and footbridge from Cromer Road.

If it's walking you like, with or without a dog, you can do no better than visit **HADLEY WOODS (Hadley Road/Northfield Road - Car Park)** where you can spends hours getting lost or watch them fishing up on Jacks Lake.

In East Barnet there is the spacious **OAK HILL PARK (Church Hill Road)** where you can play Tennis, Football, Cricket, Pitch and Putt, Bowls and it has a Children's Playground and cafe. Also the site of The East Barnet Festival.

HIGHLAND GARDENS.

It was May 1931 and Lord and Lady Hampton stand outside Highlands Garden after opening to the public the "Great Western Gateway" at Lyonsdown and the sixty-acre park at Oak Hill, which the East Barnet Urban Council acquired as a permanent open space.

The Garden was also to be opened to the public and the dignitaries were greeted by a guard of honour formed by the local fire brigade, who were to receive decorations for long service during the ceremony.

The gardens had recently been purchased by the East Barnet council as a public pleasure ground from (A Scottish banker who owned the house) "on very favourable terms". In a brief speech councillor March and said the gardens were unique and they would be a place for rest and peace for all, particularly elder people and children.

 "Here indeed is a place for peaceful recreation and I hope in the days to come it will give an opportunity for many to enjoy the beauties of nature" (Applause). Lord Hampton commended the "wonderful foresight of the council in acquiring the Highlands and Oak hill Park" He then opened the gates of the gardens and, accompanied by Lady Hampton, made a thorough inspection of the grounds. Lady Hampton was specially attracted by the lovely flowers on the terraces and by the picturesque plants that thrive in the crevices of the rocks, over which her ladyship climbed to reach the waterfall. For a few moments Lord and Lady Hampton stood on the embankment and watch the falls in silent admiration. (Barnet Press 9th May 1931)

The gardens were now open to the public but what happened after that is a mystery as not many records have been kept, probably because everyone took the house and the park for granted.

The house was demolished in 1972 and it could be the children (now adults) who played there, who might have more answers to this jigsaw.

Joseph Braithwaite's house

The Friends of Highlands Garden is a local organisation who would like to see the restoration of the gardens and, which to those that remember it had a little bit of magic.

Highlands Garden today.

The site of the old house are now flats

HISTORY OF THE BULL THEATRE.

Records of an inn on this site go back to the 1400's. The present building dates from about 1750 although Tudor timbers were found in a chimney fire in 1987. The tiling on the front with the two porches and bull's head drain spouts are Victorian, when it was known as The Old Bull.

1963. Bought by Barnet UDC for a Civic Defence Centre and perhaps as junction point for proposed ring road to allow for pedestrianisation of the High Street.

1965-1975. Became Barnet Magistrates Court Office until they moved to No.7. Meanwhile the proposal for the ring road was dropped because of opposition from the Hadley Green end.

Nov 1975 Barnet Centre Association takes on a monthly lease from the London Borough of Barnet. BCA was a community association of local societies, a registered charity formed in 1973 at a time of building boom when local halls were being sold off. BCA held an annual summer festival in Ewen Hall which continued for 10 years until 1983.

1976. Craftsmen rent upstairs rooms. Shared Experience presents "Arabian Nights", their first touring show, in the downstairs gallery where monthly crafts fairs are held.

1977. Gallery and shop are improved through a Job Creation Scheme. Small theatre created in the upstairs front rooms and weekly performances, drama courses and exhibitions begin.
1981. Development scheme approved by LBB, under the Government's Community Centre scheme with 50% grant from the Government, 25% by LBB and 25% by BCA, mostly financed through 4 – 7 year covenant payments by members.
1982. Stables in courtyard converted into 10 studio workshops for artists / craftsmen.
1984. A Manpower Services Scheme finances a team of administrators and another of building workers. Studio Theatre opens in lower floor of new block behind the original building.
1985. Graham Bennett is appointed as Centre Director with funding for a professional programme. BCA is dissolved and becomes The Old Bull Arts Association Ltd.
1988. Main Theatre upstairs is completed with assistance from the LBB and opens on 28th Feb 1988. Nick Ewbank succeeds Graham Bennett, who moves to Millfield Theatre.
1995. Alison Duthie becomes Centre Director. The programme outgrows the building
1998. Proposals for the development of former Gaumont Cinema site at Tally Ho Corner lead to plans for *arts depot* and OBAA Ltd. eventually merges with The Arts Depot Trust.
2004. Arts depot opens in the autumn and The Susi Earnshaw Theatre School become tenants of The Bull, with space continuing to be available at the evenings and weekends for theatre and community use.

History compiled by Pam Edwards, founder member and organiser up to 1985, together with Dennis O'Brien, who was Chairman and did an enormous amount to create the first small theatre. He then supervised building work, as did. Fred Fuller and Alan Cook (electrics). Gill McNeil (drama), Lesley Richardson, John Blandford and Malcolm Peters (administrators) served as original Trustees and together with Pam continue to serve on the Arts Depot Trust. Local musicians and others gave much support, including a Raising the Roof appeal in 2002.

THE WARREN THEATRE.

In 2024 the Warren amateur theatre group celebrated 75 years of preforming and raising money for local charities.

In 1949 a Mr. E.J Bunn organised a group of fellow East Barnet Royal British Legion members into a party to put on shows and pantomimes to raise money for needy ex-servicemen and their families. The group called themselves "Bunny's Warren" and "Bunny" produced the first pantomime "Dick Whittington" in St James' Hall, New Barnet in January 1950 from which a very worthwhile sum of £43 was raised for the British Legion's Not Forgotten Fund.

In 1981 they decided to branch out on their own, thus enabling the proceeds of the charity to be donated not only to the Not Forgotten Fund but also other local charities. Up until 1991 they performed their annual pantomime in the Church House Hall in Cockfosters. However 1992 saw the warren move to a "real theatre" when they performed "Frankenstein the Pantomime "at the Intimate theatre in Palmers Green.

In 2006 they moved to the Bull theatre in Barnet which is a lovely, intimate theatre where the audiences feel close to the action. Unfortunately the theatre only holds 150 people for each performance and due to the success of their pantomimed they took the decision to move to the Wyllyotts theatre in Patters Bar in 2018, so they could perform to bigger audiences and therefore raise more money for their chosen charities. The Wyllyotts is a professional local theatre with great facilities including a bar, café and disabled access.

I have seen many of their performances and have never been disappointed and neither have the audiences that they entertain so well. In 2022-2023 they raised a total of £10,300 for local charities.

So look out for their show which you can find them on their web site **www.thewarren.info** or even join the group. Brian Carroll.

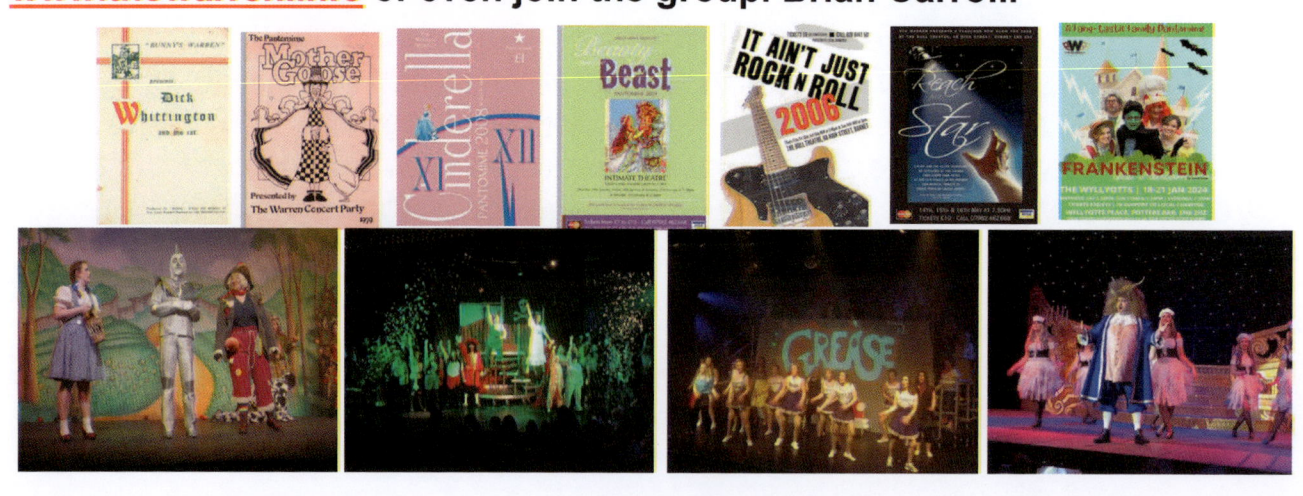

SIR ALEXANDER CUMING.
(1691 – 1775)

Did you know there is an Indian chief buried at St Mary the virgin?

Sir Alexander Cuming: 'Chief of the Cherokees' was born in Edinburgh in 1691, of Scottish nobility. When he was 12 he attained a Captain's commission from Queen Anne and he led a company during the Jacobite uprising in 1715. He had also became a lawyer and declined the Governorship of Bermuda in 1722,

In 1729 he became a member of the Royal Society of London and had been granted the King's leave of absence to travel. America was his choice to visit and in March 1730 he made the dangerous journey to the Cherokee mountains (now in South Carolina and Virginia) as a self-styled diplomat on behalf of his country although he had no authority from the King or the government.

But Sir Alexander was an independent man and his dream was to visit the people of the Cherokee people.
He must have impressed them as by the 3d of April 1730, in a general meeting of chiefs, he was crowned commander and chief ruler of the Cherokees and was presented with the scalps of their enemies.

He then set off for Charlestown arriving on April 13, with seven Indian chiefs that he was taking to London and on 5th June they arrived at Dover.

On their way to London

A few days later Cuming presented the Indians to King George II at Windsor.

Cuming saw little of the Indians during their stay where they went to the theatre, dined with bishops, were amazed at the crown jewels in the Tower of London and received an audience with the royal family, The population of the Cherokees was estimated to be around 60,000, and an alliance with the French was close to being forged but Cumings stopped that and on June 22nd 1730 a treaty was signed between the English and the Cherokee Nation (even though no such 'nation' actually existed!)

Shortly after that Sir Alexander Cuming was thrown in jail for debt and was unable to accompany the Cherokee delegation on their return trip to America. The Indians loved Cuming, and were much impressed by his imprisonment. They regarded the white men as exceedingly foolish to place a man in jail for debt, thus making it impossible for him to pay! Among them was Oukou-naka, who was later to be known as Attacullakulla (the Little Carpenter), one of the greatest Cherokee Chiefs who ever lived.

Little is known of Sir Alexander's later life although it is known he returned to the army. He died aged 84 and was buried in East Barnet churchyard on 28th August, 1775 but there is no sign of his grave which has been either damaged or, through time, the inscription has eroded.

The name of Sir Alexander Cuming may not mean anything to the people of Barnet but to the Cherokee he was an important part of their history.

WHO'S WHO IN BARNET.
SPIKE MILLIGAN.

Sir Terrance Allan 'Spike' Milligan was born in India on16th April 1918 to a father who was an Irish captain in the British army He lived in India until he was 15 and then his family moved back to England.

He joined the British army at the start of world war two, serving in the Royal Artillery. After the war he tried his luck as a musician and comedian before he teamed up with Peters Sellers and Harry Secombe to form THE GOONS.

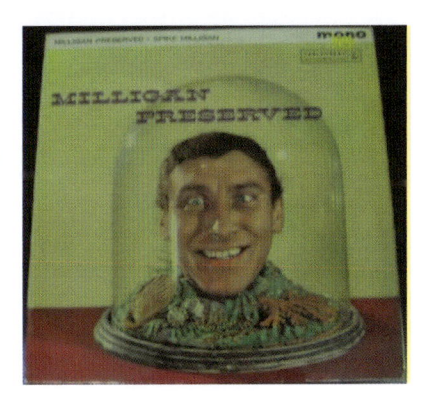

The show became a huge success, but it created enormous pressures for Milligan, which eventually led to a nervous breakdown. After The Goon Show, Spike went on to write and star in the TV sketch series Q, and published lots of written material including his famous war memoirs which began with "Hitler, my part in his downfall".

He was the favourite comic of Prince Charles and was dubbed "the godfather of alternative comedy" by Eddie Izzard, as well as inspiring The Monty Python team.

Spike Milligan pioneered the joke without a punch line, paving the way for Monty Python and all the waves of anarchic anti-format humour that followed in the 60s, 70s, 80s and 90s.

Although he fought for the British army he was refused a British passport because he was born in India and his father was Irish, Milligan took Irish citizenship instead and never forgave the British Government.

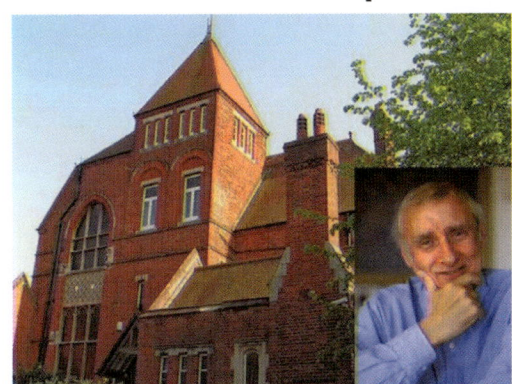

Spike was eventually made a Knight Commander of the British Empire (KBE) (honorary because of his Irish citizenship) He had been made an Honorary Commander of the British Empire (CBE) in 1992.

In a BBC poll in August 1999, Spike Milligan was voted the "funniest person of the last 1000 years".

He was also a founding member of the Finchley Society in 1971 and campaigned tirelessly to preserve Barnet's environment and its historic homes.

Milligan lived for several years in Holden Road, Finchley and moved to Monkenhurst, in The Crescent in Hadley, in 1974.

Spike spent £10,000 restoring many of its period features to their Victorian splendour, including a stained glass window depicting Barnet as one of the key sites of a battle in the Wars of the Roses.

Milligan famously entertained Prince Charles, a big fan of The Goon Show, at his family home as well as comedian Peter Sellers, who once turned up naked as a practical joke. With wit as sharp as his fellow Goon, Milligan turned the naked actor away from his door and forced him to wander the leafy streets surrounding Hadley Common.

He died from liver disease, at the age of 83, on 27 February 2002, at his home in Rye, East Sussex. The inscription on his tombstone reads "I told you I was ill" in Gaelic.

A BRIEF HISTORY OF BARNET FOOTBALL CLUB.

Barnet FC was formed in 1888 after previously being called New Barnet FC and Woodville FC. Their biggest rivals were local teams Barnet Avenue FC. and Alston Works Athletic FC. When Barnet F.C dissolved in 1901 Barnet Avenue FC renamed themselves Barnet FC and in 1912 they merged with Barnet Alston to form Barnet and Alston AFC.

On September 14th 1907 they played their first game at Underhill against Crystal Palace winning 1-0 in front of 800 spectators. In1912 they joined The Athenian league and after the war, in1919, they re-joined the league, this time, once again as Barnet F.C. The club won the league in 1931, 1932, The Forties saw success in the Herts Senior Cup, London Senior Cup and Herts Charity Cup. But their biggest triumph was in 1946, in front of 53,000 people at Stamford Bridge, beating Bishop Auckland 3-2 to lift the FA Amateur Cup.

The club again won the Athenian League the following season (1948) could not complete the double, losing at Stamford Bridge, this time to Leytonstone by 1-0. In 1959 Barnet once more reached the amateur cup final, which was now being staged at Wembley, and in an exciting final they went down as 3-2 losers to Crook Town. The club won the Athenian league again in 1964 and 1965, which was also the year they joined the southern league division two.

They won promotion to the premier league in their first season and in 1972 they were again at Wembley, this time in the F.A. Challenge cup. Once again they went home empty handed after losing 3-0 to Stafford Rangers.

They were relegated back to division 2 in 1975 but a couple of years later they were promoted again. In 1980 they joined The Alliance League which was later to be renamed The Conference League. Then in 1991 the town went crazy as we won promotion to the 4th Division (Which became the 3rd division and is now Division Two) and in 1993 they won promotion to the 2nd Division.

Barry and Stan

1992–93 season saw controversy at Underhill as Barnet chairman Stan Flashman regarding club accounts and players' wages, resulting in some nationwide back page headlines.

In spite of the financial problems, Barnet finished third in the new Division Three and secured the final automatic promotion spot to division Two. Manager Barry Fry, however, left Barnet with a handful of games remaining and was replaced by his assistant Edwin Stein, who himself then left to join Fry in the summer at Southend United

They were relegated to division Three in 1994 and after having many chances to get promoted they were relegated to the Conference in 2001. The 2004-05 season saw them promoted to League Two (the old third division) which they stayed in until 2013 when they once again returned to the Conference which did not last long and they were back in League Two for the 2005/6 season.

Jimmy Greaves Barnet FC

But by December 2011 Kleanthous became increasingly frustrated with the lack of progress from the council to extend the original lease by another 125 years. With plans to build a new stadium on the site continually rejected Kleanthous started to look elsewhere to relocate Barnet, meaning the end of their stay at Underhill.

Barnet's final game at Underhill came on 20 April 2013 against Wycombe Wanderers, which they won 1–0 in front of 6,000 spectators.

With many fans upset that the club was not only leaving the town but also going to another borough they switched their allegiance to local club, Hadley FC which is the oldest football club playing in Barnet (Founded in 1882) We end the clubs history here as like many supporters we feel the club are no longer a part of Barnet's history.

WHO'S WHO IN BARNET.
JOHN MOTSON.

OBE was born in 1945 in Salford Greater Manchester, '"Motty"', was educated at Culford School, near Bury St Edmunds, Suffolk, where, rugby, hockey and cricket were played but football was not. Motson joined the *Barnet Press* in Chipping Barnet as a junior reporter in 1963 at the age of 18 and used to report on the Barnet games.

He told the Radio Times: "I have a long connection with the club, "I was a junior reporter at the local paper (the Barnet Press) that covered their matches. I've always lived around Hertfordshire and have looked for their results ever since."
In 1965 Motson and two other local journalists formed Roving Reporter who he sometimes turned out for. They are the longest serving club and founders of the Barnet Sunday League and are still going today in the same league.

In 1968 the BBC hired him as a sports presenter on Radio 2 and three years later, he replaced Kenneth Wolstenholme at Match of the Day.
After initially having a small role on MOTD, Motson covered the famous FA cup fourth round replay between Hereford United and Newcastle on 5th February 1972, which the BBC thought would be a five minute segment following their two main games. Non-league Hereford won the match 2-1; it became the main featured game on the show and launched Motson's career.

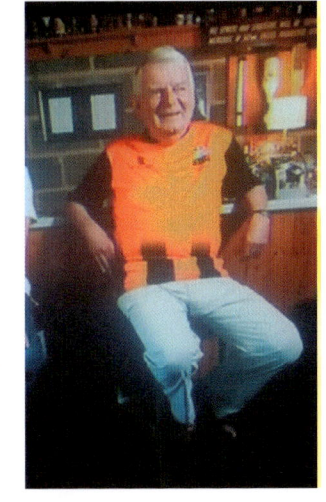

Since then he has commentated on all the major championships: World Cups, FA Cups, and European Championships. His first FA Cup Final as commentator was 1977 in the match between Manchester United and Liverpool and he was commentating on the FA Cup Semi-final of 1989 between Liverpool and Nottingham Forest when the Hillsborough Disaster occurred. Motson found himself commentating on a tragedy

~ 107 ~

rather than a football match, and he would later appear as part of the Hillsborough enquiry, since he had been a witness.
He was commentator for the 2008 European Championships Final. John Motson was famed for his sheepskin coat, which, on satirical quiz show They Think It's All Over, he revealed that he bought it off a man in Hornchurch along with 7 identical coats.
In 2008, following the BBC's loss of rights to cover live football, he announced his retirement from live commentary. The Euro 2008 final was his last live TV broadcast. He will continue to cover games for Match of the Day highlights, but will not, for instance, commentate on the 2010 World Cup in South Africa.
He died on 23 February 2023, at the age of 77

John Motson
1945-2023

WHO'S WHO AROUND BARNET
SPORT

DENNIS BERGKAMP:
Football genius who played for Arsenal and Holland lived in Cockfosters. Played for Ajax and Inter Milan before joining Arsenal in 1995. He was named the FWA Footballer of the Year and PFA Players' Player of the Year in April and May 1998. Bergkamp also achieved a unique feat in being voted first, second and third on Match of the Day's Goal of the Month competition in August 1997. For his national team, Bergkamp was the joint top scorer at Euro 1992[and was selected in the All-Star team for the tournament, an honour he also received at the Cup. He retired from football in 2006.

DAVID GINOLA: lived in Totteridge. He is a French former professional footballer who has also worked as an actor, model and football pundit. A forward, Ginola played for ten seasons in France with Toulon, RC Paris, Brest and Paris Saint-Germain before moving to Newcastle United in the English Premier League in July 1995. He subsequently played for Tottenham Hotspur, Aston Villa and Everton before retiring in 2002. At international level, he made 17 appearances, scoring three goals, for the France national team between 1990 and 1995.

GEORGE GRAHAM: Former Arsenal and Tottenham manager lived in Cockfosters. He made 455 appearances in England's Football League as midfielder or forward for Aston Villa, Chelsea, Arsenal, Manchester United, Portsmouth and Crystal Palace. He also managed Millwall, Leeds United and Tottenham Hotspur. But it is player and manager at Arsenal that he will always be remembered for his laid back style of play which earned him the nickname "Stroller". He played 308 matches for Arsenal, scoring 77 goals. And as manager he won between 1987 and 1995, two league titles (1989 and 1991), the 1993 FA Cup, two Football League Cups (1987 and 1993), and 1994 European Cup Winners' Cup.

LENNOX LEWIS: Heavyweight Champion of the World lived in Hadley. He is a former professional boxer who competed from 1989 to 2003. He is a three-time world heavyweight champion, a two time lineal champion, and at the time of writing the last heavyweight to hold the undisputed championship. He is regarded by many as one of the greatest heavyweight boxers of all time, and one of the greatest British fighters of all time. He vacated his remaining titles and retired in 2004 with a record of 41 wins (32 by knockout), 2 losses, and 1 draw.

ARSENE WENGER: Manager of Arsenal lived in Totteridge. He was the manager of Arsenal from 1996 to 2018, where he was the longest-serving and most successful in the club's history. His contribution to English football through changes to scouting, players' training, and diet regimens revitalised Arsenal and aided the globalisation of the sport in the 21st century. He won the FA Premier League 3 times (1997–98, 2001–02, 2003–04) the FA Cup 7 times (1997–98, 2001–02, 2002–03, 2004–05, 2013–14, 2014-15, 2016-17) and the FA Community Shield 5 times (1998, 1999, 2002, 2004, 2014, 2015) He is currently serving as FIFA's Chief of Global Football.

BILLY WRIGHT: Ex England Captain. Lived in Lyonsdown Road. He played as a centre half and he spent his entire club career at Wolverhampton Wanderers. The first footballer in the world to earn 100 international caps, Wright also held the record for longest unbroken run in competitive international football, with 70 consecutive appearances, He made a total of 105 appearances for England, captaining them a record 90 times,

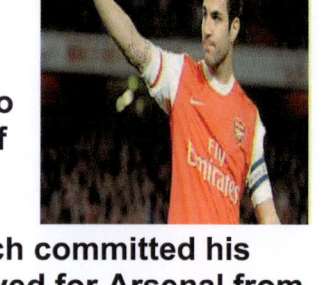

CESC FABREGAS Lived in Lyonsdown road.
Fàbregas came through Barcelona's youth academy, leaving at 16 when he was signed by Arsenal in September 2003. He went on establish himself in the team. He broke several of the club's records in the process, earning a reputation as one of the best players in his position, and won the FA Cup in 2005. He was also named in the UEFA Team of the Year twice and the PFA Team of the Year twice. He became Arsenal's youngest-ever first team player, aged 16 years and 177 days. He signed his first professional contract with Arsenal in September 2004, which committed his long-term future to the club. In October 2004. The Spaniard played for Arsenal from 2003-11 and picked up just one trophy in that time, the 2005 FA Cup, before he left for Barcelona. He made 110 appearances for Spain, helping them capture the World Cup and the European Championships twice. He lived in club digs in with a family in Lyonsdown road when he first came to the club.

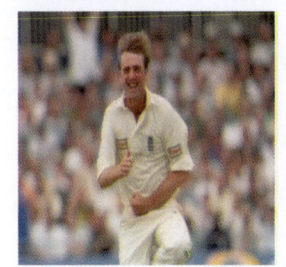

PHIL TUFNELL was born in Barnet in 1966 and is a former English international cricketer and current television and radio personality. He played in 42 Test matches and 20 One Day Internationals for the England cricket team, as well as playing for Middlesex County Cricket Club from 1986 to 2002. Tufnell took 121 Test match wickets. His Test average is 37.68 per wicket. Across all first-class cricket he took over 1,000 wickets at an average of 29.35. His cheerful personality and behaviour have made him a popular sports personality. Following his retirement from playing cricket in 2002, Tufnell has built on his popularity with several television appearances, including They Think It's

All Over, Celebrity Deal Or No Deal, A Question of sport, Strictly Come Dancing, and winning I'm a Celebrity Get Me Out of Here! He used to live in Cockfosters.

DARREN BARKER lived in Mays Lane and is a British former professional boxer who competed from 2004 to 2013. He held multiple titles at middleweight, including the IBF title in 2013; the Commonwealth title from 2007 to 2009; the British title in 2009; and the European title from 2010 to 2011. As an amateur, Barker represented England at the 2002 Commonwealth Games and won a gold medal in the light-welterweight division. On 17 August 2013, Barker challenged Australian Daniel Geale for the IBF Middleweight world title. Despite being knocked down by his Australian opponent in the sixth round by a vicious body shot Barker battled back and won his first world title taking a split decision victory.

In early Autumn 2013, it was announced by Eddie Hearn that Barker's first defence of the IBF Middleweight Title would be against veteran German boxer Felix Sturm at the Porsche-Arena, Stuttgart, Germany on 7 December 2013. Felix Sturm dropped and felled Barker twice in the second round before his corner threw in the towel, Barker having dislocated his hip from the first knockdown. Following the fight, Barker spoke about retirement due to a recurring hip injury and eventually in 2014 he announced his retirement from boxing.

MUSIC

EMMA BUNTON (Baby Spice) born in Barnet, (21 January 1976) and lived in Finchley and went to St Theresa's Roman Catholic Primary School. Her parents, Pauline, karate instructor, and Trevor a milkman, split when she was 11, after which she stayed with her mother. She rose to fame in the 1990s as a member of the pop girl group the Spice Girls, in which she was nicknamed Baby Spice, reflecting the fact that she was the youngest member. With over 100 million records sold worldwide, the group became the best-selling female group of all time. The Spice Girls achieved a total of 9 UK Number 1 ones.

LEE THOMPSON: Sax Player with Madness lives in Barnet. Thompson came to prominence in the late 1970s as a founder and saxophonist for the English ska band Madness. founded Madness with Mike Barson and Chris Foreman in 1976, and wrote the group's debut single, "The Prince". Among the other songs, he wrote or co-wrote the singles "Embarrassment", "House of Fun", and "Uncle Sam". Thompson was featured floating while playing a red, white, and blue-coloured saxophone in the closing ceremonies of the 2012 Summer Olympics Madness have had 16 singles reach the UK top ten, including "One Step Beyond", "Baggy Trousers", "It Must Be Love", one UK number-one single "House of Fun" In 1984, Thompson married Debbie (née Fordham). They have three children named Tuesday, Daley and Kye.

On 23rd July 2013 Lee opened the Barnet Music Festival by playing at the top of Barnet Church, the highest point to York in the north and the Ural mountains in the east. This was followed by his band The Silencerz (featuring his son Daley) playing In the Church below.

PAUL YOUNG: Popular Singer lived in Hadley and East Barnet Born 17 January 1956 he formerly the frontman of the short-lived bands Kat Kool & the Kool Cats, Streetband and Q-Tips, he became a teen idol with his solo success in the 1980s. His hit singles include "Love of the Common People", "Wherever I Lay My Hat", "Come Back and Stay", "Every Time You Go Away" and "Everything Must Change", all reaching the top 10 of the UK Singles Chart. Released in 1983, his debut album, No Parlez, was the first of three UK number-one albums.

BEVERLEY SISTERS: were an English female close harmony pop vocal trio, consisting of three sisters from London, Joy and twins Teddie. They were most popular during the 1950s and 1960s and their most successful records were of Christmas songs, including I Saw Mommy Kissing Santa Claus (1953), and Little Donkey and Little Drummer Boy (both 1959). The sisters were each appointed MBE in 2006. Joy was married to footballer Billy Wright and lived in Lyonsdown Road, New Barnet. The sisters were often seen around Barnet

CLIFF RICHARD: Legendary "young one" and Shadows front man lived in Totteridge.
He had 67 UK top ten singles, the second highest total for an artist (behind Presley). He holds the record, with Presley, as the only act to make the UK singles charts in all of its first six decades (1950s–2000s).

PETER BANKS, (15 July 1947 – 7 March 2013), Born and grew up in Barnet, where he attended Barnet Secondary School and Barnet College of Further Education. He played rhythm with local Barnet group the Nighthawks, then on leaving school joined the Devil's Disciples and made his first records with them in 1964. He was the original guitarist in the rock band Yes, and has been described as "the architect of progressive music".

AMY WINEHOUSE was an English singer and songwriter and born on 14 September 1983 at Chase Farm hospital in Enfield. Her family lived in the Southgate where she attended Osidge Primary School and then secondary at Ashmole School. In 1992, her grandmother suggested that Amy attend the Susi Earnshaw Theatre School, where she went on Saturdays to further her vocal education and to learn to tap dance. She attended the school for four years and founded a short-lived rap group called Sweet 'n' Sour. In July 2000, she became the featured female vocalist with the National Youth Jazz Orchestra. Winehouse's best friend, soul singer Tyler James, sent her demo tape to an A&R person and the rest is history.

In 2008 she won five prizes at the Grammy Awards, including Song of the Year and Record of the Year (both for her single "Rehab"), and Best New Artist. Winehouse died of alcohol poisoning in 2011 at age 27.

STEVE ELLIS (born 7 April 1950) lived in Finchley and went to Bishop Douglas School. He is an English rock/pop singer. In the late 1960s. He formed his first band as the lead vocalist, which was called Soul Survivors when he was fifteen. The Soul Survivors formed into Love Affair in 1966. A few months later, in early 1967, the band released their first two singles, including "Everlasting Love", a song that knocked The Beatles' "Hello, Goodbye" off the number one spot on British charts. Love Affair would go on to have more commercial success, with songs such as "A Day Without Love", "Rainbow Valley", and "Bringing on Back the Good Times". In 2022 Steve released a solo album called "Finchley Boys"

ART and LITTRATURE

KINGSLEY AMIS: English novelist, poet, critic and teacher. He wrote more than 20 novels, He wrote Lucky Jim and The Old Devils. His biographer Zachary Leader called him "the finest English comic novelist of the second half of the twentieth century." In 2008, The Times ranked him ninth on a list of the 50 greatest British writers since 1945. He lived with his wife Elizabeth Jane Howard in Hadley wood in the 70s

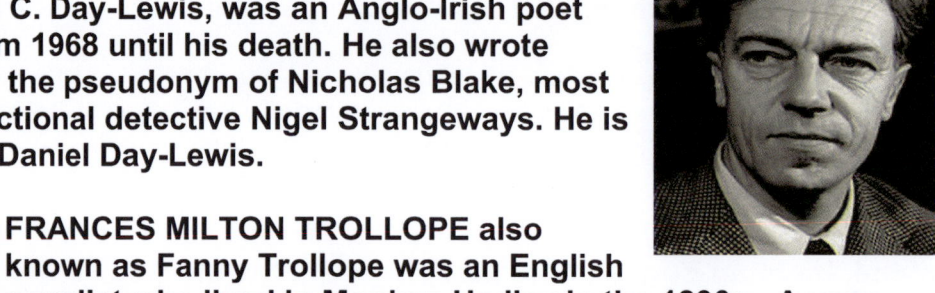

CECIL DAY-LEWIS 27 April 1904 – 22 May 1972), often written as C. Day-Lewis, was an Anglo-Irish poet and Poet Laureate from 1968 until his death. He also wrote mystery stories under the pseudonym of Nicholas Blake, most of which feature the fictional detective Nigel Strangeways. He is the father of actor Sir Daniel Day-Lewis.

FRANCES MILTON TROLLOPE also known as Fanny Trollope was an English novelist who lived in Monken Hadley in the 1830s. A very famous writer in her day her book, Domestic Manners of the Americans (1832) observations from a trip to the United States, is the best known. She also wrote social novels: one against slavery is said to have influenced Harriet Beecher Stowe, and She wrote 40 books: six travelogues, 35 novels, countless controversial articles, and poems. In 1843, Frances visited Italy and eventually moved to Florence permanently and died there in 1863,

BEN WILSON was born in Cambridge and grew up in Barnet. North London, Ben began creating large wood sculptures: outsized human figures, still lifes, tables and chairs. During his art foundation course at Middlesex Polytechnic he seized the opportunity to construct the first of his many art environments, large-scale structures that you can climb on or walk inside in the wooded area behind the college building. Wooden figures were surreptitiously positioned around Barnet with works created in nearby woodlands (Hadley wood) using wood from fallen trees. From October 2004, chewing gum art became his principal focus as he started work on a vast sequence of gum pictures that began in Barnet High Street and would eventually touch most of North London and beyond. It would be the first of Ben's many chewing gum trails, the most celebrated of which are the trails (2011 to the present) that cross the Millennium Bridge from the St Paul's side and go into Tate Modern.

Thanks to my friend Mick Page for drawing my attention to this local artist

FILM.

SEAN BEAN: Star of the Sharpe TV series and Lord of The Rings, lived in Totteridge.
His film roles include Patriot Games (1992) Golden Eye (1995), The Lord of the Rings trilogy (2002). He also stared as Ned Stark in the award winning series Game of Thrones

TREVOR HOWARD: A great film actor with more than 100 screen credits including Brief Encounter (1945), Mutiny on The Bounty (1962), Ryan's Daughter (1970) The Charge of the Light Brigade (1968), Battle of Britain (1969), and Gandhi lived in Arkley and The Gate pub was his local. For his performance in Sons and Lovers (1960) he was nominated for the Academy Award for Best Actor. Howard died aged 74, at his home in Arkley, on 7 January 1988. The cause of death was hepatic failure and cirrhosis of the liver

NORMAN WISDOM lived in Galley Lane, Barnet.
He was an English actor, comedian, musician and singer best known for a series of comedy films produced between 1953 and 1966 featuring a hapless character called Norman Pitkin.
He was awarded a Knighthood by the Queen in 2000:
He died on 4 October 2010 on the Isle of Man at the age of 95.

TERRY THOMAS was born in Nether street North Finchley. He was an English character actor and comedian who became internationally known through his films during the 1950s and 1960s. He often portrayed disreputable members of the upper classes, especially cads, toffs and bounders, using his distinctive voice; his costume and props tended to include a monocle, waistcoat and cigarette holder. His striking dress sense was set off by a ⅓-inch (8.5 mm) gap between his two upper front teeth. Stared in It's a Mad, Mad, Mad, Mad World Those Magnificent Men in Their Flying Machines and Monte Carlo or Bust!

ROGER MOORE: The James Bond actor lived in Totteridge when he was making The Saint TV series at Borehamwood. He went on to play James Bond in Live and Let Die, The Man with the Golden Gun, The Spy Who Loved Me, Moonraker, For Your Eyes Only, Octopussy and his final appearance as 007 in A View to a Kill.

SHOW BUSINESS.

JEREMY BEADLE MBE (12 April 1948 – 30 January 2008)
He was an English television presenter, radio presenter, writer and producer. From the 1980s to the late 1990s he was a regular face on British television, and in two years appeared in 50 weeks of the year. Beadle become nationally famous as one of the presenters of LWT's Game for a Laugh, the first programme made by ITV to beat the BBC's shows in the Saturday night ratings battle.[4] This was followed by a hidden-camera style practical joke show, Beadle's About (1986–1996), which became the world's longest continuously running hidden-camera show.
From 1990 to 1997, Beadle presented You've Been Framed!, a family show featuring humorous clips from viewers' home video recordings. In the 2001 New Year Honours Beadle was made a Member of the Order of the British Empire (MBE) for his services to charity. On 25 January 2008, it was reported that Beadle had been admitted to a north London hospital, and was subsequently placed in a critical care unit with pneumonia. He died on 30 January 2008 at the age of 59.

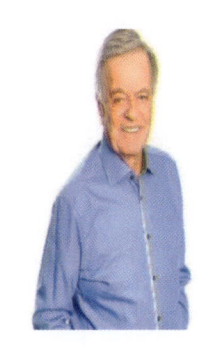

TONY BLACKBURN: Popular DJ lives in Arkley.
He first achieved fame broadcasting on the pirate stations Radio Caroline and Radio London in the 1960s, before joining the BBC, on the BBC Light Programme. He was the first disc jockey to broadcast on BBC Radio 1 at its launch, on 30 September 1967, and has had several stints working for the corporation. He has also worked for Capital London, Classic Gold Digital and London. Blackburn has won two lifetime achievement awards from the Radio Academy, the second of which was to mark his fifty years of broadcasting. In 2023, Blackburn launched the digital music channel That's 60s, focusing on 1960s music. On 2 January 2023, in the month in which he celebrated his 80th birthday, Blackburn presented a two-hour slot, "Your Soul Mate" for BBC Radio 2, sharing his favourite genre of music and his personal memories associated with the playlist.
In April 2023 Blackburn took a leave of absence from his radio work and other work commitments due to ill health. He fully recovered and resumed his radio work.

CAROL HAWKINS: born in Barnet (31 January 1949) is an English actress, best known for her various comic roles in numerous television sitcoms and films in the 1970s and 1980s. She played the roles of Sharon Eversleigh in the film of the television series Please Sir! The Fenn Street Gang and Sandra in the BBC TV series Porridge, and starred in two Carry On films (Carry On Abroad and Carry On Behind. She performed in British comedy films of the 1970s, such as two Carry On films: Carry On Abroad (1972), and Carry On

Behind (1975), Hawkins "retired" in 2005, with the aim of devoting more time to spiritual matters and animal care and has her own web site.

SIR DAVID JASON, Britain's most popular actor lived at Lodge Lane, North Finchley and attended nearby Northside School. He joined Incognitos (a local theatre group in Holly Park Road, Friern Barnet) in his mid-teens and that was the start of his acting career.

He has played Derek "Del Boy" Trotter in the BBC sitcom Only Fools and Horses, Detective Inspector Jack Frost in A Touch of Frost, Granville in Open All Hours and Still Open All Hours, and Pop Larkin in The Darling Buds of May, as well as voicing several cartoon characters, including Mr. Toad in The Wind in the Willows, the BFG in the 1989 film, and the title characters of Danger Mouse and Count Duckula.

In September 2006, Jason topped the poll to find TV's 50 Greatest Stars, as part of ITV's 50th anniversary celebrations. He was knighted in 2005 for services to acting and comedy. Jason has won four British Academy Television Awards (BAFTAs), (1988, 1991, 1997, 2003), four British Comedy Awards (1990, 1992, 1997, 2001) and seven National Television Awards (1996 twice, 1997, 2001 twice, 2002 and 2011).

ELAINE PAIGE OBE (born 5 March 1948) is an English singer and actress, best known for her work in musical theatre. Raised in Barnet she attended Southaw Girls' School in Oakleigh Park the Aida Foster Theatre School, making her first professional appearance on stage in 1964 at the age of 16. Her appearance in the 1968 production of Hair marked her West End debut. Following a number of roles over the next decade, Paige was selected to play Eva Perón in the first production of Andrew Lloyd Webber's Evita in 1978, which brought her to the attention of the broader public. For this role, she won the Laurence Olivier Award for Performance of the Year in a musical.

She originated the role of Grizabella in Cats and had a Top 10 hit with "Memory", a song from the show. In 1985, Paige released "I Know Him So Well" with Barbara Dickson from the musical Chess, In addition to being nominated for five Laurence Olivier Awards. She has released 22 solo albums, of which eight were consecutively certified gold and another four multi-platinum.

DANIEL PEACOCK: Comedian/Actor who starred in the film Party Party lived Barnet, and he attended Ashmole School in Southgate. After working as a Bluecoat at Pontins he moved into acting and writing and his credits as an actor include the following television series: , The Young Ones, , Only Fools and Horses, Robin of Sherwood, The Bill, Doctor Who Casualty and One Foot in the Grave. His film appearances include Porridge, Quadrophenia, Gandhi, Party Party, Bull in Robin Hood: Prince of Thieves, and Carry On Columbus. He also played young Jacques Clouseau in Trail of the Pink Panther and he appeared in The Jewel of the Nile as the special effects maestro.

In 2016, Peacock played the role of Maurice in Spencer Hawken's No Reasons. Since around 2019, Peacock has been working as a carer at Hastings Court Care Home in East Sussex, resulting in a nomination for a National Care Award in 2022.

PETER SELLERS CBE (Who used to live in Whetstone) was an English actor and comedian. He first came to prominence performing in the BBC Radio comedy series The Goon Show and became known to a worldwide audience through his many film roles, among them Chief Inspector Clouseau in The Pink Panther series. Perhaps the best way of artistic range include I'm All Right Jack (1959), Dr. Strangelove (1964), What's New Pussycat? (1965), Casino Royale (1967), The Party (1968), Being There (1979) and five films of the Pink Panther series (1963–1978). Sellers' versatility enabled him to portray a wide range of comic characters using different accents and guises, and he would often assume multiple roles within the same film. Sellers was nominated three times for an Academy Award, twice for the Academy Award for Best Actor, for his performances in Dr. Strangelove and Being There, and once for the Academy Award for Best Live Action Short Film for The Running Jumping & Standing Still Film (1959). He won the BAFTA Award for Best Actor in a Leading Role twice, for I'm All Right Jack and for the original Pink Panther film, The Pink Panther (1963), and was nominated as Best Actor three times. In 1980 he won the Golden Globe Award for Best Actor – Motion Picture Musical or Comedy for his role in Being There. In his personal life Sellers struggled with depression and insecurities and he frequently clashed with his directors and co-stars, especially in the mid-1970s, when his physical and mental health, together with his alcohol and drug problems were at their worst. Sellers was married four times and had three children from his first two marriages. He died from a heart attack, aged 54, in 1980.

STEPHANIE BEACHAM (born 28 February 1947) English actress born in Barnet, she, attended the Queen Elizabeth's Girls' Grammar School in Barnet. In a career spanning almost six decades, she has a wide number of credits to her name on film, television, stage and radio in both the United Kingdom and the United States. She appeared in numerous films such as her screen debut in the 1970 film The Games following this with The Ballad of Tam-Lin (1970) The Nightcomers. By the mid-1970s, Beacham had become widely known for her roles in British horror films including Dracula A.D. 1972 (1972), And Now the Screaming Starts! (1973) and House of Mortal Sin (1975),
But it was Beacham's role as Sable Colby in the ABC series Dynasty (1985–1989) and its spin-off The Colbys (1985–1987) that would make her a household name on both sides of the Atlantic. She was nominated for a Golden Globe Award in 1990 for her role in Sister Kate, as well as several other nominations for playing Sable Colby in The Colbys and Dynasty.
Beacham returned to television in the UK playing Phyl Oswyn in the ITV prison-based drama series Bad Girls (2003–2006), Martha Fraser in Coronation Street (2009, 2022), and Maureen in the BBC sitcom Boomers (2014–2016), as well as venturing into reality television competing on Strictly Come Dancing (2007) and Celebrity Big Brother (2010).

101 THINGS ABOUT BARNET.

1. High Barnet founded by monks from St Albans Abbey in the 12th Century.
2. In 1196. Barnet was known as "Bernet".
3. King John granted Barnet a market charter in 1199.
4. A Chapel was built on site of Barnet Church in 1250.
5. In 1219. Barnet was known as "Barnatt".
6. The First reference to East Barnet was in 1249.
7. The First reference to Chipping Barnet was in 1329.
8. In 1420 St Johns Church (Barnet Church) was extended.
9. Barnet Fair and market were granted a charter by Queen Elizabeth I in 1588.
10. The Great North Road built through Barnet in the 17th Century. It was the main coach route from London to Scotland.
11. Samuel Pepys visits the Barnet physic well in 1667.
12. The Hadley Highstone obelisk is erected in 1740.
13. Market day is changed from Monday to Wednesday in 1758. The fair changed from April to September.
14. The first stage coach service through Barnet opened in1784.
15. In 1870 the last horse race in Barnet, "The Barnet Stakes" was held where High Barnet station now stands.
16. Hadley Brewery closed down in 1969.
17. The gold doorknob in Barnet church is supposed to be in line with the cross on top of St Paul's cathedral.
18. On the eve of the Battle of Barnet in 1471, 3 kings slept in the town of Barnet Edward IV, Henry VI and the Duke of Gloucester, who later became Richard III.
19. It was reported in the Times that in September 1834 Barnet fair was the largest cattle market in England, with up to 40,000 animals on offer and £100,000 being taken in trade on the first day.
20. In 1349 84 Barnet residents died of the Black Death, a plague that swept Europe.
21. Warwick the Kingmaker, who died at the Battle of Barnet, was the second richest man in the country (after the king).
22. The top of Barnet church is the highest point to the Ural Mountains in the east and York to the north.
23. Barnet won the FA Amateur cup in 1946.
24. The first 35mm was made and shown in Barnet by Birt Acres.
25. The Well house Hospital is renamed Barnet Hospital in the 1950s.

26. The East Barnet Festival is the largest free festival in London.
27. The oldest pub in Barnet is The Kings Head in the High Street (1626). The Mitre is the second oldest (1633). This is according to Richard Selbys excellent book "Barnet Pubs – Another Round"
28. The famous explorer David Livingstone lived in Hadley.
29. The oldest church is St Mary the Virgin in East Barnet.
30. New Barnet station opened in 1850.
31. The Prince of Wales pub in East Barnet dates back to 1876.
32. Mallard, the fastest steam train in the world used to pass through New Barnet station.
33. Barnet Museum was opened in March 1938.
34. The Bells Hill Cemetery contains 45 Commonwealth War Graves. 17 of them are from the Second World War.
35. The Clash and the Dammed used to play at the Duke of Lancaster (now flats at the back of Sainsburys).
36. In the 1850's a William Aldridge purchased some land near the railway station and decided to build a hotel. As there was another hotel called the Railway Hotel already built nearby he decided to call his the Railway Tavern.
37. Lee Thompson of Madness lives in Barnet.
38. The original Cat and Lantern used to be on Cat Hill.
39. Spires was opened on May 1989.
40. General William Booth, founder of the Salvation Army, lived in Hadley Wood from 1889 until his death in 1912.
41. The site of Spires used to be a church.
42. Stephanie Beecham was born in Barnet.
43. There could be up to 10,000bodies buried after the Battle of Barnet but nobody knows where they are.
44. Emma Bunton was born in Barnet.
45. The Bull Theatre building dates back to about 1750.
46. More than 10,000 people attend the East Barnet Festival.
47. The cockney rhyming slang for hair is "Barnet" after our Barnet Fair.
48. Charles Dickens used to drink at the Red Lion. He heard that his wife had given birth to a daughter here.
49. Samuel Pepys used to visit the Physic well in Well road.
50. Barnet hill was built in 1827.
51. Before Barnet Hill was built the road into Barnet went pass the Old Red Lion and came out at Victoria Lane.
52. The Battle of Barnet was listed in the top ten battlefields by the Sunday Times.
53. Sainsburys in New Barnet was opened on the 30 September 1980.
54. There used to be a cinema where Budgens in the village now stands.

55. During World War II a bomb nearly hit the museum in Wood Street.
56. General Monck is reputed to have stayed at the Mitre in 1660.
57. 150 coaches used to travel through Barnet High Street in the 18th century.
58. There has been a fair in Barnet since Queen Elizabeth I granted a charter in 1588.
59. According to Charles Dickens Oliver Twist met the Artful Dodger near Victoria Bakers in the High Street.
60. Barnet is mentioned in H. G. Wells "The War of the Worlds"
61. Barnet football club was formed in 1888.
62. The film "Party Party" was filmed in Lytton Road and New Barnet
63. Barnet Odeon was built in 1935 and is a Grade II listed building,
64. The Tudor Hall dates back to 1577.
65. Elizabeth I is said to have stayed in Barnet and would have passed through the town travelling between Hatfield House and London.
66. Chipping (as in Chipping Barnet) means Market.
67. The Cat and Lantern in the village, the Bell and Buck and the Duke of Lancaster in New Barnet and the Green Man in the High Street are no longer there. All these were music pubs.
68. Kitts End Lane used to be the main road to Holyhead.
69. The oldest school in Barnet is Queens Elizabeth school for boys (1573)
70. Paul Young lived in New Barnet.
71. The St Albans Road was built in 1828.
72. There used to be a cinema in Barnet High Street.
73. The ghost of Geoffrey de Mandeville is supposed to haunt Oakhill Park.
74. Did you know we had another museum in Barnet? It was called the Abbey folk park. In 1934 John Ward established an open-air museum at Hadley Hall, 89 Park Road, New Barnet which featured a prehistoric village, a 13th-century tithe barn from Kent, and a 17th-century well. The Princesses Elizabeth and Margaret were among its many visitors. In May 1945 Ward was charged with enticement and went bankrupt. He went abroad shortly afterwards.
75. Kingsley Amis (the author of "Lucky Jim) lived in Hadley.
76. The Poet Laureate C. Day-Lewis died at the home of author Kingsley Amis in Hadley in 1972? He was the father of actor Daniel Day-Lewis.
77. On September 1st 1909, a Miss Frances Trehearn opened St Catherine's school in Stapylton Road and two years later there were 62 children being taught there - 27 boys and 35 girls.
78. In May 1931 and Lord and Lady Hampton opened Highlands Garden in New Barnet.

79. At the time of publishing (2024) The Warren amateur dramatic group have been preforming for charity for 75 years.
80. EBOGS (East Barnet Old Grammarians) was formed in 1948 and resulted directly from the efforts of Mr. Allan Clayton, the first headmaster of East Barnet Grammar.
81. Livingstone School opened in January 1954.
82. The famous actor Trevor Howard lived in Arkley.
83. Norman Wisdom lived in Arkley.
84. The Salisbury in the High Street was demolished in 1988. The sign is in the Barnet Museum.
85. The borough was named Barnet in 1965 and we still wonder why they chose us instead of Hendon.
86. Jeremy Beadle used to live in Hadley.
87. Originally known as The Hadley Wood Hotel (now the Hadley hotel) there has been a public house on this site since 1861.
88. Battle of Barnet fought at Hadley during the Wars of the Roses in 1471.
89. Oakleigh Park Station opens in 1873.
90. The Barnet Cinema built was built in 1913 (On the site of the current post office in the High Street).
91. In 1935 a lorry killed four people at Barnet Fair.
92. High Barnet station becomes part of the London Underground in 1940.
93. The Well house Hospital was renamed Barnet Hospital in the 1950s.
94. Spires shopping centre opened in 1989.
95. The old fire station near Lytton Road closed in 2005.
96. Barnet reached the third round proper of the FA Cup for the first time on 9 January 1965, meeting the previous season's runner-up Preston North End at Underhill. 2–0 down inside the first 10 minutes, the second half saw Barnet, urged on by 10,500 spectators, level the score at 2–2, before a last minute own goal sent them out.
97. In October 1946, the first live televised football match was broadcast by the BBC from Underhill.
98. A police station was opened at the junction of Edward and Margaret Roads in 1884, with one inspector, three sergeants, and 15 constables, but was closed in 1933, and the building demolished in 1985.
99. Comic Genius Spike Milligan lived in Hadley.
100. The most senior officer to survived the sinking of the Titanic, Charles Lightoller lived in Hadley.
101. www.Barnet 4U is the best historic site about the town.

Printed in Great Britain
by Amazon